Divorce
in Washington

The Legal Process,
Your Rights, and What to Expect

David J. Crouse

Addicus Books
Omaha, Nebraska

An Addicus Nonfiction Book

ISBN 978-1-938803-82-6
Typography Jack Kusler

This book is not intended to serve as a substitute for an attorney. Nor is it the author's intent to give legal advice contrary to that of an attorney. The information contained in this book is for general informational purposes only and should not be relied upon or considered legal advice applicable to a specific legal matter.

Library of Congress Cataloging-in-Publication Data

Crouse, David J., 1965- author.
  Divorce in Washington : the legal process, your rights, and what to expect / David J. Crouse.
      pages cm
  Includes index.
  ISBN 978-1-938803-82-6 (alk. paper)
1. Divorce—Law and legislation—Washington (State)—Miscellanea. I. Title.
  KFW100.C76 2014
  346.79701'66—dc23

                                        2013036768

                    Addicus Books, Inc.
                     P.O. Box 45327
                   Omaha, Nebraska 68145
                   www.AddicusBooks.com

              Printed in the United States of America
                   10 9 8 7 6 5 4 3 2 1

*To my clients. Facing family law litigation is always a
daunting endeavor. For their trust in me to successfully guide
them through this process, I am grateful. We started as attorney
and client, and ended as friends.*

Contents

Acknowledgments

I was very fortunate to have the benefit of extraordinary mentors early in my legal career. Prior to my first year in law school, I was hired as a law clerk by Edward Goss, a partner in the Spokane, Washington firm of Goss, Hipperson & Sampson. Except for some experience as a police officer, I had no legal training. Yet, for some reason, Ed decided to take a chance on me. During my next three years of law school, Ed devoted himself to teaching me civil procedure and courtroom decorum. I learned what it meant to be a professional. Ed modeled integrity every day that I worked for him, and I deeply respected him.

Ed's partner Linnwood Sampson was equally influential. Linn was one of those rare individuals that allowed me to actually work his cases and trusted who I would properly perform the tasks assigned. He didn't check up on me, but he set his expectations high. Linn would not accept second rate work. Thanks to Linn, I graduated law school with more courtroom and law practice experience than many second-or third-year attorneys. Although Linn practiced primarily in the area of real estate law, he took on many divorce and other family law cases exclusively to allow me the opportunity of working on them before I graduated from law school. Linn's generosity and guidance was exceptional and never forgotten.

The third firm partner, Brian Hipperson, showed me how to run a business. Law school does not teach how to properly manage a firm. Fortunately for me, Brian was an able teacher. The lessons I learned from Brian are still being applied in my law office management to this very day.

I owe an enormous debt of gratitude to the Honorable Wm. Fred Aronow (Ret.). Before Fred was appointed to the Superior Court bench, he practiced divorce and family law, sharing office space with Goss, Hipperson & Sampson. When I expressed a strong interest in family law during law school, Fred began sharing his forms, files, and expertise with me. Fred gave me complete access to his office, allowing me to freely tap twenty years of experience. Fred even took the time to introduce me to Superior Court judges, court staff, and other family law attorneys. My career advanced rapidly because of Fred's efforts. He proved to be the consummate friend and mentor.

I don't know if I have ever properly thanked Ed, Linn, Brian, and Fred. I hope that they know how much their mentoring has meant to me. I think about all of them often. If they have any question about how influential they have been to me, I trust that this acknowledgment answers those questions.

Success in professional life is often the result of strong family support. That has certainly been true for me. I could not imagine more supportive parents than my parents James and JoAnn Crouse. They shepherded me carefully through school, and fully stood by me when I decided to leave college to fulfill a personal desire to serve my country in the military and to serve my community as a police officer. When I completed my quest and returned to college, they were there to back me in every way possible. Without my loving parents, I seriously doubt that I would be writing this book today. Thank you for all that you have done.

Building a quality law practice is a sacrifice. Forty hour workweeks are a fantasy: Eighty-or ninety-hour workweeks are the usual rule at the outset of a practice. This sacrifice was shared by my family. I can't imagine traveling this road without my wife of twenty-six years, Cherie. She handled everything while I was gone. She is a wife, mother, and friend without equal. I look forward to wherever our future journeys will take us.

Finally, I would be very remiss if I did not thank my alma mater Gonzaga University and the Gonzaga University School of Law. You not only welcomed me after having been recently discharged from my military service, but you generously provided me with scholarships to fund my undergraduate

Acknowledgments

education. If this was not enough, you provided me with a full scholarship to law school based primarily on my military and police service. Gonzaga University is the embodiment of the Jesuit tradition of service. Go Zags.

David J. Crouse
Attorney at Law

Introduction

Facing a divorce is one of life's ultimate challenges. It has been said only the loss of a child is more stressful. I believe this to be true.

Whether you initiate or respond to a divorce, you are facing a change in every single part of your life. No area remains untouched from a divorce action. Parenting, family relationships, finances, social networks, personal belongings, a residence, and job performance are all affected by a divorce. My purpose in writing *Divorce in Washington* is to help you navigate through an uncertain journey.

Divorce is hard. I see my courageous clients, like you, making tough decisions every day in the face of their changing worlds. I know from my experience in representing literally thousands of clients over the years, it can take a tremendous amount of support and guidance to successfully navigate the divorce journey. *Divorce in Washington* was written to help you move through this time of transition with more clarity and ease. It is not intended to be a substitute for advice from your attorney. Rather, it is designed to assist you in partnering with your attorney to reach your goals in the resolution of your divorce.

In *Divorce in Washington,* I endeavor to partner with you and explain each step in your divorce process in the hope that it will lead to your empowerment. The more control and clarity you feel over the process, the better you are able to make sound decisions regarding very challenging choices. I hope you will use this book as a guide to ask your attorney questions, to understand what it is you are unclear about, and to begin to see the big picture of the journey upon which you are about to embark.

I hope this book will be used not only by people going through divorce, but also by the professionals who support you—attorneys, mediators, therapists, clergy, financial advisors, and others who are called upon to serve people who are divorcing. Although every divorce is different and its circumstances unique, I hope that *Divorce in Washington* will endeavor to answer your multitude of questions as you begin this road toward a new beginning. Inevitably, you will begin to see the new possibilities for your future.

1

Understanding the Divorce Process

At a time when your life can feel like it is in chaos, sometimes even the smallest bit of predictability can bring a sense of comfort. The outcome of many aspects of your divorce may be unknown, but quality advice and guidance can provide much-needed clarity. While initially intimidating, there is one part of your divorce that does have some measure of predictability, and that is the divorce process itself.

Most divorces proceed in a step-by-step manner. Despite the uniqueness of your divorce, you can generally count on one phase of your divorce following the next. Sometimes simply realizing you are completing stages and moving forward with your divorce can reassure you it will not go on forever.

Develop a basic understanding of the divorce process. This will lower your anxiety when your attorney starts talking about "depositions" or "going to trial." It can reduce your frustration about the length of the process because you understand why each step is needed. It will allow you to begin preparing for what comes next. Most importantly, understanding the divorce process will make your journey easier. Who wouldn't prefer that?

1.1   What is my first step?

Find a law firm that handles divorces as a regular part of its law practice. Firms that practice exclusively in the area of family law are highly desirable. You can find firms that focus on family law throughout Washington.

Personal referrals can be very helpful. The best recommendations come from people who have personal knowledge of an attorney's experience and reputation. Referrals from court personnel, other attorneys, mediators, and others with a legal background are often of the highest quality. Financial advisors or accountants can also be a great referral source.

Even if you are not ready to file for divorce, call to schedule an appointment right away to obtain information about protecting yourself and your children. This is especially true if you sense that your spouse might be getting ready to pursue a divorce. Ask what documents you should take to your initial consultation. Make a list of your questions to bring to your first meeting. Start making plans for how you will pay your attorney to begin work on your case.

1.2   Must I have an attorney to get a divorce in Washington?

You are not required to have an attorney to obtain a divorce in Washington. However, if your case involves children, significant property or debts, professional practices or businesses, or spousal maintenance, you should avoid proceeding on your own. Where the issues are more complex, the failure to secure an attorney can have potentially disasterous and long-lasting consequences. Good counsel is an exceedingly good investment.

Even if your divorce does not involve any of these issues, still strongly consider contacting an attorney. Washington divorce law can be exceedingly complex. There are many issues, both positive and negative, that you might not even be aware of. If you are considering proceeding without an attorney, at a minimum have an initial consultation with an attorney to discuss your rights and duties under the law. Meeting with an attorney can help you decide whether to proceed on your own.

If meeting with an attorney is not a viable option for you, seek guidance from other sources. Call your local courthouse to see whether there is a family law facilitator available to provide assistance. The county bar association is a great resource and often coordinates free advice clinics or free (*pro bono*) representation. Call them. The Washington law schools also provide representation for qualified individuals through law clinics. A person who proceeds in a legal matter without an attorney is referred to as being *pro se,* meaning on one's own.

Steps in the Divorce Process

- Obtain a referral for a lawyer.
- Schedule an appointment with an attorney.
- Prepare questions and gather needed documents for the initial consultation.
- Meet for the initial consultation with attorney.
- Pay retainer to attorney and sign retainer agreement.
- Provide requested information and documents to your attorney.
- Take other actions as advised by attorney, such as opening or closing financial accounts.
- Attorney prepares petition for dissolution (divorce) and supporting documents for your review and signature.
- Attorney files petition for dissolution with clerk of the court. Attorney obtains *ex parte* restraining orders if appropriate. Attorney obtains hearing date for temporary matters.
- Mandatory ninety-day waiting period begins when other spouse is served or signs an acceptance of service.
- Negotiations begin regarding terms of temporary order on matters such as custody, support, and temporary possession of the family home. Attorneys prepare declarations, financial affidavits, and child-support worksheets for temporary hearing.
- Temporary hearing is held.

OR

- Parties reach agreement on temporary order.
- Temporary order is prepared by one attorney, approved as to form by other attorney, and submitted to the judge for signature.
- If there are minor children, parties must attend a parent education class, develop a parenting plan, or participate in mediation as required by their particular county.

- Both sides conduct discovery to obtain information regarding all relevant facts. If needed, obtain valuations of all assets, including expert opinions.
- Confer with attorney to review facts, identify issues, assess strengths and weaknesses of case, review strategy, and develop proposal for settlement.
- Spouses, guided by their attorneys, attempt to reach agreement through written proposals, mediation, settlement conferences, or other negotiation.
- Parties reach agreement on all issues.
- Attorney prepares decree of dissolution and required supporting court orders for approval by spouses and attorneys.

OR

- Certificate of readiness for trial is filed with court asking that a trial date is set or a trial date is set by the court pursuant to a case scheduling order.
- Pay trial retainer to fund the work needed to prepare for trial and services for the day or days of trial.
- Parties prepare for trial on unresolved issues.

OR

- Trial preparations proceed and include the preparation of witnesses, trial exhibits, legal research on contested issues, pretrial motions, trial brief, preparation of direct and cross-examination of witnesses, preparation of opening statement, subpoena of witnesses, and closing argument to the court.
- Meet with attorney for final trial preparation.
- Trial is held.
- Judge makes decision.
- Attorney prepares decree.
- Other attorney approves decree as to form.
- Decree submitted to judge for signature.
- Judge signs decree of dissolution. Make payments and sign documents (deeds or titles) pursuant to decree.

- Documents required to divide retirement accounts and ensure the payment of child support are submitted to the court.
- Pay any remaining balance due on attorney's fees or receive refund.

1.3 Is Washington a *no-fault* state or do I need grounds for a divorce?

Washington, like most states, is a *no-fault* divorce state. This means that neither you nor your spouse are required to prove the other is "at fault" in order to be granted a divorce. Factors such as infidelity or abandonment are not necessary to receive a divorce in Washington. Rather, it is only necessary for a spouse to state that the marriage is "irretrievably broken" in order to have it dissolved.

Although not required, if your case proceeds to a final trial, then the brief testimony of either you or your spouse is sufficient evidence for the court to rule that the marriage should be dissolved. This testimony will simply state that the marriage is irretrievably broken. The judge is unlikely to ask for any further information as to this issue. If your case settles prior to trial, this "irretrievably broken" language is simply inserted into your final documents and no testimony is required from either you or your spouse.

1.4 How will the judge view my or my spouse's infidelity?

Because Washington is a no-fault divorce state, there will rarely be testimony or evidence introduced about either spouse's infidelity. Generally, the judge will hear testimony regarding an extramarital affair only if it is relevant to the case. Infidelities may become relevant where community assets or funds are transferred to this other individual, where sexual conduct has occurred in front of the child, where the child suffers from exposure to this other party, or where the other person has a background that includes criminal activity or domestic violence that could endanger the child. Ask your attorney if the infidelity could be relevant.

1.5   Do I have to get divorced in the same state I married in?

No. Regardless of where you were married, you may seek a divorce in Washington if the jurisdictional requirements of residency are met. The jurisdictional requirements are discussed in the following question.

1.6   How long must I have lived in Washington to get a divorce in the state?

Washington does not have a minimum residency requirement. Washington only requires that you are actually residing (domiciled) in the state, with the intent to remain a resident of the state. However, just because you *can* file in Washington does not always mean that this is your best option. If you have recently moved to Washington and your spouse resides in another state, you should discuss with an attorney the issue of where to file your divorce. This is especially true if you have real property (house or land), children, or significant assets in that other state. Under certain circumstances, more than one state can have jurisdiction to grant you a divorce.

1.7   Can I divorce my spouse in Washington if he or she lives in another state?

Provided you are a resident of Washington, you can file for divorce here even if your spouse lives in another state. However, as discussed in question 1.6 above, Washington may or may not be the best state to file in under these circumstances. Discuss with your attorney the facts that will need to be proven and the steps necessary to give your spouse proper notice to ensure that the court will have jurisdiction over your spouse. Your attorney can counsel you on whether it is possible to proceed with the divorce in Washington.

1.8   My spouse has told me that she will never "give" me a divorce. Can I get one in Washington anyway?

Yes. Washington does not require that your spouse agree to a divorce. If your spouse threatens to not "give" you a divorce, know that in Washington this is an idle threat without any basis in the law. At most, an uncooperative spouse can only delay the divorce by not agreeing to orders and forcing a court hearing. Even then, the courts work to ensure the divorce is timely completed. If you have concerns your spouse will try to delay the divorce, talk with your attorney about ways to reduce or eliminate any delay tactics your spouse may attempt.

1.9 Can I get a divorce even when I don't know where my spouse is currently living?

Washington law allows you to proceed with a divorce even if you do not know the current address of your spouse. First, take action to attempt to locate your spouse. Contact family members, friends, former coworkers, or anyone else who might know your spouse's whereabouts. Utilize resources on the Internet that are designed to help locate people.

Let your attorney know of the efforts you have made to attempt to find your spouse. Inform your attorney of your spouse's last known address, as well as any work address or other address where this person may be found. Once your attorney attempts to give notice to your spouse without success, it is possible to ask the court to proceed with the divorce by giving notice through publication in a newspaper or by serving the spouse through certified mail.

Personal service on your spouse is always the best option. Personal service means that an appropriate individual, defined as a competent adult who is not a party to the action, physically hands the documents to the spouse. If you must proceed with service by publication or mail, seek the advice of an attorney. Service by publication or mail (often referred to as *alternate service)* is truly a trap for the unwary. The rules for this kind of service are very strict and rigidly enforced, and failure to strictly follow these rules can delay your divorce or even invalidate all or part of the divorce action. Talk to your attorney about your options and rights if you don't know where your spouse is living.

1.10 I just moved to a different county within the state of Washington. Do I have to file in the county where my spouse lives?

You may file your petition for dissolution either in the county where you reside or in the county where your spouse resides. In fact, Washington law allows you to file in any county of the state regardless of which county you reside in. However, just because you can file in any county does not mean it is advisable to do so. If a court were to find that the county in which you filed is an "inconvenient venue," it can move your case to a more appropriate county.

Generally, it is best to file in the county that has the most significant contact with your marriage. If the children are located in a particular county, if the family home is located in a particular county, or if the majority of significant assets are located in a particular county, that county is often the best county to file in. Of course, there are always exceptions. If you reside in a different county than your spouse, it is best to discuss with an attorney which county is most appropriate and beneficial to file in.

1.11 I immigrated to Washington. Will my immigration status stop me from getting a divorce?

If you meet the residency requirements for divorce in Washington, you can get a divorce in this state regardless of your immigration status. However, you should first talk to your immigration attorney about the likelihood of a divorce leading to immigration challenges. You do not want to endanger your immigration status by an improperly timed divorce filing.

If you are a victim of domestic violence, tell your attorney. You may be eligible for a change in your immigration status under the federal *Violence Against Women Act*. The existence of domestic violence may allow you to file for divorce sooner without risking your immigration status. Again, discuss this with your immigration attorney and your divorce attorney before filing for divorce. It is best if both attorneys are in contact with one another, carefully planning a time line for filing for divorce.

1.12 I want to get divorced in my Indian tribal court. What do I need to know?

Each tribal court has its own laws governing divorce. Requirements for residency, grounds for divorce, and the laws regarding property, spousal maintenance, and children can vary substantially from state law. Some tribes have very different laws governing the grounds for your divorce, removal of children from the home, and cohabitation.

Contact an attorney who is knowledgeable about the law in your tribal court for legal advice on pursuing a divorce in your tribal court or on the requirements for recording a divorce obtained in state court with the clerk of the tribal court. Many divorce attorneys who are extremely skilled in representing clients in state courts have little or no experience in tribal courts. There may also be particular reasons you should not file in tribal court which an attorney could explain to you.

1.13   Is there a waiting period for a divorce in Washington?

Yes. Washington has a mandatory ninety-day waiting period. This waiting period begins when the divorce action has been filed with the court and the *respondent,* (the person who did not initiate the divorce process), is determined to have been given legal notice of the divorce. This date of legal notice is either the day the respondent is served the divorce documents or the date the respondent signs a voluntary "Acceptance of Service" form acknowledging that he or she has been provided with the divorce documents that were filed with the court. If you have been required to serve the divorce petition by publication or mail due to an inability to locate your spouse, discuss with your attorney when the ninety-day waiting period begins as the start date can vary.

1.14   What is a *divorce petition*?

A *divorce petition,* also referred to as a "petition for dis-solution of marriage" is a document signed by the person fil-ing for divorce and filed with the clerk of the court to initiate the divorce process. The petition will set forth in very general terms what the *petitioner* (the person filing the divorce) is ask-ing the court to order.

1.15   My spouse said she filed for divorce last week, but my attorney says there's nothing on file at the courthouse. What does it mean to "file for divorce?"

When attorneys use the term "filing," they are ordinarily referring to filing a legal document at the courthouse, such as delivering a petition for dissolution to the clerk of the court. Sometimes a person who has hired an attorney to begin a divorce action uses the phrase "I've filed for divorce," although no papers have yet been taken to the courthouse to start the legal process.

1.16 If we both want a divorce, does it matter to the judge who files?

No. In the eyes of the court, the petitioner (the party who files the complaint initiating the divorce process) and the respondent (the other spouse) are not seen differently by virtue of which party filed. The court, as a neutral decision maker, will not give preference to either party. Both parties will be given adequate notice and each will have a chance to be heard and present argument. However, as discussed below, filing first can have tactical advantages even though the assigned judge will remain neutral and unbiased.

1.17 Are there advantages to filing first?

There certainly can be. There can also be advantages to waiting. Discuss with your attorney whether there are any advantages to you filing first. Your attorney may advise you to file first or to wait until your spouse files, depending upon the overall strategy for your case and your circumstances.

Since this is a frequently asked question, some examples are in order. For example, hypothetically assume that your spouse is a physician. He or she has moved out of the house and is transferring $10,000 per month to you voluntarily. Your attorney may advise you that if this matter went to court, you would get less money. It would then be advantageous to wait to file and let your spouse set a favorable precedent for you. The court may likely follow this favorable precedent if it has been in place long enough.

However, let us say that this same spouse stopped sending $10,000 per month and started sending only $1,000 per month or nothing at all. Your attorney would likely advise you to file immediately so you can receive the necessary funds to support your household. If you delayed in filing, you may set a bad precedent. It may appear you were able to make ends meet on this lesser amount, and the court may award you a lower amount of support than you actually need.

Filing first may also be necessary if your spouse will not voluntarily move out of the home and the stress of residing together becomes unbearable.

The spouse who files first, gets the benefit of presenting evidence and testimony first and last (called *rebuttal*) at trial. All of us have been previously involved in serious discussions. Ask yourself, "Is it beneficial to have first and last say in these discussions?" Of course it is. The same benefit applies to your divorce action. However, there may be benefits to waiting that outweigh the obvious benefits of filing first. Allow your attorney to support you in making the decision about whether and when to initiate the legal process by filing a petition for dissolution of marriage.

1.18   Can I stop the newspaper from publishing notice of the filing or granting of my divorce?

Generally, the answer is no. Documents filed with the court, such as a divorce petition or a final decree, are matters of public record. Newspapers have a right to access this information, and many newspapers publish this information as a matter of routine. There is no set schedule to determine when this information will be published. Contact your attorney or local newspaper to learn more.

If the filing of a divorce is likely to cause you substantial professional or personal harm, talk with your attorney about filing the divorce petition in a different county. Divorces filed in a different county would not ordinarily appear in your local newspaper. For example, attorneys from all over Washington sometimes may file their petitions in Lincoln County due to Lincoln County's favorable filing rules, which allow attorneys to mail in court orders rather than personally appear to present them to the judge. However, while such actions may avoid newspaper publishing, they can increase the cost of the divorce due to the travel required if hearings become necessary. Also, a court may move your case to a different county if it finds the current county to be inconvenient. Discuss these issues carefully with an attorney.

1.19 Is there a way to avoid embarrassing my spouse and not have the sheriff or process server serve him with the divorce papers at his workplace?

Talk to your attorney about the option of having your spouse sign a document known as an *Acceptance of Service.* The signing and filing of this document with the court can eliminate the need to have your spouse served by the sheriff or by a private process server. By signing this form, your spouse only acknowledges that he or she received the filed divorce documents.

Another way to avoid having your spouse personally served is to make arrangements to have him or her pick up the divorce documents at your attorney's office. After your spouse picks up the documents, your attorney or a member of his or her staff will submit an *Affidavit of Service.* Remember: because you are a party to the action, you cannot serve your spouse.

The use of an Acceptance of Service is not appropriate for all cases. An Acceptance of Service should probably not be used when a spouse is likely to evade service, when restraining orders are necessary, when a spouse may try to hide or conceal assets when given notice, or when there is a need to get to a temporary orders hearing quickly. Discuss with your attorney the better choice for your case.

1.20 Should I sign the Acceptance of Service form even if I don't agree with what my spouse has written in the petition for divorce?

Signing the Acceptance of Service does not mean you agree with anything your spouse has stated in the divorce petition or anything your spouse is asking for in the divorce. Signing this form is simply a substitute for having a sheriff or private process server hand you the documents personally. You do not waive the right to object to anything your spouse has stated in the petition for dissolution of marriage.

However, you must be careful to determine if the form also contains a *joinder section.* If there is a joinder section contained in the acceptance of service document, and you signed the form, you would be stating that you agree to everything contained in your spouse's petition for dissolution. This could have very negative consequences for you. You could be bound by the terms contained in the petition for dissolution, even if you later discover that these terms were very unfair. Further, in many cases, signing a joinder could also mean that your spouse could enter final divorce documents without further notice to you so long as these orders contained the same terms as the petition for dissolution. Accordingly, it is not advisable to sign such a document without first discussing it with your attorney.

There could be other reasons why you would not want to sign this form. Follow your attorney's advice on whether and when to sign an Acceptance of Service form.

1.21 Why should I contact an attorney right away if I have received divorce papers?

If your spouse has filed for divorce, it is important that you obtain legal advice as soon as possible. Even if you and your spouse are getting along, having independent legal counsel can help you make decisions now that could affect your divorce later. The actions you take in the weeks after the divorce is filed, as to visitation, personal conduct, and financial matters, can have very long-term consequences. In fact, some decisions may have such negative consequences that your attorney will never be able to fully resolve them.

After your spouse has filed for divorce, a *temporary orders hearing* can be scheduled at any time. A temporary orders hearing is set by filing a motion for temporary orders. At the hearing, the judge can enter orders for a temporary parenting plan, a temporary order of child support, temporary maintenance, temporary debt division, interim occupancy of the family home, use of property, attorney fees, necessary restraining orders, and other issues. It is possible you will receive only a few days' notice of a temporary orders hearing. You will be better prepared for a hearing if you have already retained an attorney. Further, after you have been served with the petition for dissolution, a written answer responding to your spouse's divorce petition must be filed with the court within twenty days if you were served within the state of Washington. Other time lines will apply if you are served outside the state of Washington, by publication, or by certified mail. Discuss this with your attorney.

1.22   What is an *ex parte court order*?

An *ex parte court order* is obtained by one party going to the judge to ask for something without giving prior notice or an opportunity to be heard by the other side. Usually, emergency restraining orders are sought with an *ex parte* court order, but emergency child custody and use of property are also sought with *ex parte* orders. With the exception of restraining orders, judges are reluctant to sign *ex parte* orders. Ordinarily the court will require the other side to have notice of any requests for court orders, and a hearing before the judge will be held.

Before a judge will sign an *ex parte* order, an *affidavit,* which is a written statement sworn under oath, is usually required. Generally, *ex parte* orders are limited to emergency situations, such as requests for temporary restraining orders and protection orders. These orders can remove a spouse from a home without notice, eliminate all contact between the spouse and their children without notice, or grant other relief. If there is a concern that your spouse will begin transfer assets upon learning about your plans for divorce, your attorney might advise you to seek a temporary restraining order to protect against such an action, without giving prior notice to your spouse. This may also be advised if there is any potential for domestic violence.

When an *ex parte* order is granted, the party who did not request the order will have an opportunity to have a subsequent hearing before the judge to determine whether the order should remain in effect. Some counties will allow this hearing to occur very quickly. If you have been served with an *ex parte* order, it is extremely important that you immediately meet with an attorney to quickly resolve any loss of your rights, which has likely occurred.

1.23   What is a *motion*?

A *motion* is a request that the judge enter a court order of some type. For example, your attorney may file a written motion with the court asking for an order related to temporary custody, child support, parenting time/residential time, or financial matters, such as payment of bills. Some motions are made to handle certain procedural aspects of your case, such as a motion for a continuance asking that a court date be changed or a motion for extension of time asking that the court extend a deadline.

1.24 Once my petition for divorce is filed, how soon can a temporary hearing be held to decide what happens with our child and our finances while the divorce is pending?

Each county determines how much notice is required for a temporary orders hearing. Some counties will allow hearings with just five days-notice. Other counties require ten days-notice. In emergency situations, the court may allow a hearing with only hours of notice.

Be aware that the other spouse's attorney may ask for a continuance of the hearing in order to properly prepare. Courts frequently grant the first request for a continuance unless an emergency exists or there are other time-sensitive issues. Subsequent continuance requests become more difficult to obtain. Usually, a temporary hearing can be held within thirty days of your divorce being filed with the court, assuming your spouse can be located to be given notice.

1.25 How much notice will I get if my spouse seeks a temporary order?

It depends on the request. For example, if there is an emergency regarding the children where harm may occur to them if the hearing is delayed, a court may allow a hearing on just a few hours of notice. This is fairly rare. Depending on the county you reside in, five to ten days-notice (or more) can be expected. Discuss with your attorney the notice requirements of the county you have filed in.

1.26 During my divorce, what am I responsible for doing?

Your attorney will explain what actions you should take to further the divorce process and to help you reach the best possible outcome.

You will be asked to:

- Keep in regular contact with your attorney.
- Update your attorney regarding any changes in your contact information, such as your address, phone number, and/or e-mail address.

- Provide your attorney with all requested documents.
- Provide requested information in a timely manner.
- Complete forms and questionnaires.
- Appear in court on time.
- Be direct about asking any questions you might have.
- Tell your attorney your thoughts on settlement or what you would like the judge to order in your case.
- Remain respectful toward your spouse throughout the process.
- Keep your children out of the litigation.
- Comply with any temporary court orders, such as restraining or support orders.
- Advise your attorney of any significant developments in your case.

By doing your part in the divorce process, you enable your attorney to partner with you for a better outcome while also lowering your attorney fees.

1.27 I'm worried that I won't remember to ask my attorney about all of the issues in my case. How can I be sure I don't miss anything?

Write down all of the topics you want to discuss with your attorney, including what your goals are for the outcome of the divorce. The sooner you determine your goals for the outcome of your divorce, the easier it will be for your attorney to support you to get what you want. However, there is no reason to agonize over all potential details and issues. Realize that your attorney will think of some issues that you may not be thinking of and will probably cover all of the issues that are important to you during your consultation and subsequent meetings. Your attorney's experience will be helpful in making sure nothing important is forgotten; this is another reason why it is important to select an attorney whose practice has a family law focus.

Divorce Issues Checklist

	Notes
Dissolution of marriage	
Custody of minor children	
Removal of children from jurisdiction	
Parenting plan	
Child support	
Deviation from child support-guidelines	
Abatement of child-support/residential credit	
Travel expenses to facilitate parenting time for out-of-state parents	
Life insurance to fund unpaid child support	
Automatic withholding for support	
Child-support arrearage from temporary order	
Child-care expenses	
Child-care credit	
Health insurance on minor children	
Uninsured medical expenses for minor children	
Extracurricular expenses for children	
Private school tuition for children	
College expenses for children	
College savings accounts for the benefit of children	
Health insurance on the parties	
Real property: marital residence	
Real property: rentals, cabins, commercial property	
Time-shares	
Retirement accounts	
Federal or military pensions	
Business interests	
Bank accounts	

Divorce Issues Checklist (Continued)

	Notes
Investments	
Stock options	
Stock purchase plans	
Life insurance policies	
Life insurance to secure alimony	
Frequent-flyer miles	
Credit card points	
Season tickets for events	
Premarital or nonmarital assets	
Premarital or nonmarital debts	
Pets	
Personal property division: including motor vehicles, recreational vehicles, campers, airplanes, collections, furniture, electronics, tools, household goods	
Exchange date for personal property	
Division of marital debt	
Property settlement	
Spousal maintenance	
Life insurance to fund unpaid maintenance	
Arrearage of spousal maintenance from temporary order	
Tax exemptions for minor children	
IRS Form 8332	
Filing status for tax returns for last/current year	
Former name restoration	
Attorney fees	

1.28 My spouse has all of our financial information. How will I be able to prepare for negotiations and trial if I don't know the facts or have the documents?

Once your divorce has been filed with court and temporary matters have been addressed, your attorney will proceed with a process known as *discovery*. Through discovery, your attorney can ask your spouse to provide documents and information needed to prepare your case. Your attorney can also subpoena information directly from an institution to obtain the requested documentation. One of the first documents that your attorney will likely serve is interrogatories. *Interrogatories* ia a list of written questions that must be answered under oath. This is a common form of discovery and one that is quite cost-effective.

1.29 My spouse and I both want our divorce to be amicable. How can we keep it that way?

You and your spouse are to be acknowledged for your willingness to cooperate while focusing on moving through the divorce process. This will not only make your lives easier and save you money on attorney fees, but it is also more likely to result in an outcome with which you are both satisfied. Find an attorney who understands your goal to reach settlement and encourage your spouse to do the same.

Cooperate with the prompt exchange of necessary information. Then ask your attorney about the options of mediation and negotiation for reaching agreement. Even if you are not able to settle all of the issues in your divorce, these actions can increase the likelihood of agreement on many of the terms of your divorce decree.

However, be careful to follow your attorney's advice. Some clients, despite the best of intentions, can negatively affect their case by being too anxious to settle. Time may be needed to properly value assets and assess the most effective strategy. Time may also be needed to see how children adjust to the new parenting schedule. If your attorney advises you to engage in further evaluation before settling, give this advice great consideration.

1.30   Can I pick my judge?

You will generally not be able to pick your own judge. In many counties, a judge is assigned to the case at the time of filing. Some counties only have one or two judges. There are situations, however, where your attorney may be able to schedule a motion before a particular judge. Additionally, Washington law allows a party to file an *affidavit of prejudice* which removes one judge from your case. There are restrictions and time lines on filing an affidavit of prejudice, so carefully discuss this with your attorney.

Talk to your attorney about the reasons you want a different judge. Other options may be available. For example, if you believe that your judge has a conflict of interest, such as being a close friend of your spouse, you may have a basis for asking the judge to "recuse" him or herself in order to allow another judge to hear the case.

1.31   How long will it take to get my divorce?

The more you and your spouse are in agreement, the faster your divorce will conclude. At a minimum, there will be a ninety-day wait from the date of the filing of the petition for dissolution and service of the divorce petition on the non-filing spouse. Most divorces, however, do not conclude at the ninety-day mark.

Assuming all issues, such as custody, support, property, and debts, are completely settled between you and your spouse, you can complete the final decree and supporting documents and enter them with the court any time after the ninety-day period. However, if you cannot come to an agreement on all issues, a trial will be scheduled to complete your divorce on these unresolved issues. The time required to get to a trial can vary widely by county.

Some counties can get you to trial soon after the ninety-day period has expired. This is the exception rather than the rule, though. Many counties schedule trial about ten to twelve months after the divorce petition was filed. If a county has a greater backlog, the wait can be even longer.

1.32   What is the significance of my divorce being final?
The finality of your divorce decree, referred to as the *decree of dissolution of marriage*, is important for many reasons. It allows you to remarry, affects your eligibility for health insurance from your former spouse (often terminating it), and affects your filing status for income taxes. Continuing health insurance is an issue that must be discussed with your attorney.

1.33   When does my divorce become final?
Your divorce becomes final when your judge signs the divorce decree. Don't assume that the judge has signed the decree just because it was left with him or her. Ensure you receive a copy of the signed decree and carefully check the date placed on the order by the judge.

1.34   Can I start using my former name right away and how do I get my name legally restored?
You may begin using your former name at any time, provided you are not doing so for any unlawful purpose, such as to avoid your creditors. Many agencies and institutions, however, will not alter their records without a court order changing your name. If you want your former name restored, let your attorney know so that this provision can be included in your divorce decree. If you want to change your legal name after the divorce and have not provided for it in your decree, it will be necessary for you to undergo a separate legal action for a name change.

2

Coping with Stress during the Divorce Process

It may have been a few years ago or it may have been many years ago. Perhaps it was only months. But, when you said, "I do," you meant it. Like most people getting married, you planned to be a happily married couple for life.

But things happen. Life brings change. People change. Whatever the circumstance, you now find yourself considering divorce. The emotions of divorce run from one extreme to another as you journey through the process. You may feel relief and ready to move on with your life. On the other hand, you may feel emotions that are quite painful such as anger, fear, sorrow, or a deep sense of loss or failure. Remember, it is important to find support for coping with all these strong emotions.

Because going through a divorce can be an emotional time, having a clear understanding of the divorce process and what to expect will help you make better decisions. When it comes to decision making, try to clarify your intentions and goals for the future. Nobody expects that you will have these answers right away. Your attorney and your judge will understand that you need time. As time passes, things will become increasingly clearer for you, especially if you have the benefit of a good attorney.

2.1   My spouse left home weeks ago. I don't want a divorce because I feel our marriage can be saved. Should I still see an attorney?

It's a good idea to see an attorney. Whether you want a divorce or not, there may be important actions for you to take now to protect your assets, credit, home, children, and any future right to obtain support. If your spouse files for divorce, a temporary hearing could be held in a matter of days. It is best to be prepared with the support of an attorney, even if you decide not to file for a divorce at this time.

Additionally, it is very difficult to see things clearly when a separation occurs or a divorce is filed. Emotions cloud your view. This happens to everyone. Because your view is clouded, your decisions may not be the best ones for your situation. This is another reason to quickly meet with an attorney, so you may receive unbiased advice and guidance.

2.2   The thought of going to an attorney's office to talk about divorce is more than I can bear. I canceled the first appointment I made because I just couldn't do it. What should I do?

Many people going through a divorce are dealing with attorneys for the first time and feel anxious about the experience. Ask a trusted friend or family member to go with you. He or she can support you by writing down your questions in advance, taking notes for you during the meeting, and helping you to remember what the attorney said after the meeting is concluded. It is very likely you will feel greatly relieved just to be better informed.

2.3   There is some information about my marriage that I think my attorney needs, but I'm too embarrassed to discuss it. Must I tell the attorney?

Your attorney has an ethical duty to maintain confidentiality. He or she is obligated to keep private past events in your marriage you may share. Attorneys who practice divorce law are accustomed to hearing intimate information about families. Although it is deeply personal to you, it is unlikely anything you tell your attorney will be a shock.

It may feel uncomfortable for a short moment, but it is important that your attorney have complete information so your interests can be fully protected. If speaking directly about these facts still seems too difficult, consider putting it in a letter. Your attorney will respect your willingness to be open and candid.

2.4   I'm unsure about how to tell our children about the divorce, and I'm worried I'll say the wrong thing. What's the best way?

How you talk to your children about the divorce will depend upon their ages and development. Changes in your children's everyday lives, such as a change of residence or one parent leaving the home, are important to them. Information about legal proceedings and meetings with attorneys are best kept among adults.

Simpler answers are best for young children. Avoid giving them more information than they need. Use the adults in your life as a source of support to meet your own emotional needs.

After the initial discussion, keep the door open to further talks by creating opportunities for your children to talk about the divorce. Use these times to acknowledge their feelings and offer support. Always assure them that the divorce is not their fault and that they are still loved by both you and your spouse, regardless of the divorce.

2.5   My youngest child seems very depressed about the divorce, the middle one is angry, and my teenager is skipping school. How can I cope?

A child's reaction to divorce can vary depending upon his or her age and other factors. Some may cry and beg for reconciliation, while others may behave inappropriately. Reducing conflict with your spouse, being a consistent and nurturing parent, and making sure both of you remain involved are all actions that can support your children regardless of how they are reacting to the divorce.

Support groups for children whose parents are divorcing are also available at many schools and religious communities. A school counselor may also provide support. If more help is needed, confer with a therapist experienced in working with

24

children. Talk with your attorney about whether it is advisable to place your child in counseling. Your ability to do so, without the express agreement of your spouse, may be impacted or restricted if a parenting plan or other orders have been entered in your case.

2.6 I am so frustrated by my spouse's "Disneyland parent" behavior. Is there anything I can do to stop this?

Feelings of guilt, competition, or remorse may tempt a parent into spending parenting time on trips to the toy store or other special activities. These feelings may result in an absence of discipline in an effort to become the favored parent or to make the time "special." Such conduct is very frustrating.

Shift your focus from the other parent's behavior to your own, and do your best to be an outstanding parent during this time. This includes keeping a routine for your child for family meals, bedtimes, chores, and homework. Encourage family activities, as well as individual time with each child, when it's possible. If you feel the other parent's conduct is sabotaging your relationship with your children, discuss this with your attorney. There are times the conduct of the other parent becomes so extreme that court intervention is necessary.

During the time when a child's life is changing, providing a consistent and stable routine in your home can ease his or her anxiety and provide comfort. Your own counselor can suggest other strategies specific to your situation. In the long run, your children will benefit from your efforts to bring stability to an otherwise uncertain situation.

2.7 Between requests for information from my spouse's attorney and my own attorney, I am totally over-whelmed. How do I manage gathering all of this de-tailed information by the deadlines imposed?

First, simply get started. Make this a priority. Often thinking about a task is worse than the task itself.

Second, break it down into smaller tasks. Perhaps one evening gather your tax returns, and on the weekend work on your monthly living expenses.

Third, let in support. Ask that friend of yours who just loves numbers to come over for an evening with her calculator to help you get organized. Family members can be very helpful. Sometimes, it is advisable to have them spend time with your children in order to give you the time you need.

Finally, communicate with your attorney. Your attorney or paralegal may be able to make your job easier by giving you suggestions or help. The paralegal can take a more active role while still not dramatically increasing your attorney fees. It may also be that essential information can be provided now, with details submitted later.

2.8 I am so depressed about my divorce that I'm having difficulty getting out of bed in the morning to care for my children. What should I do?

See your health care provider. Feelings of depression are common during a divorce. You also want to make sure to identify any physical health concerns.

Although feelings of sadness are common during a divorce, more serious depression means it is time to seek professional support. Your health and your ability to care for your children are both essential. Follow through on recommendations by your health care professionals for therapy, medication, or other measures to improve your wellness. Keep your attorney informed of your situation.

2.9 Will taking prescribed medication to help treat my insomnia and depression hurt my case?

Not necessarily. Talk to your health care professional and follow their recommendations. Taking care of your health is of utmost importance during this difficult time, and will serve your best interests as well as the best interests of your children. Inform your attorney of any medications you are taking or treatment that you are seeking.

2.10 I know I need help to cope with the stress of the divorce, but I can't afford counseling. What can I do?

You are wise to recognize that divorce is a time for letting in support. You can explore a number of options, including:

- Meeting with a member of the clergy or lay chaplain
- Joining a divorce support group

- Turning to friends and family members
- Going to a therapist who offers counseling services on a sliding-fee scale
- Discussing with your attorney whether spousal maintenance can be ordered or increased

If none of these options are available, look again at your budget. You may see that counseling is important enough that you decide to find a way to increase your income or lower your expenses to support this investment in your well-being. This is an area that can justify the use of credit.

2.11 I'm the one who filed for divorce, but I still have loving feelings toward my spouse and feel sad about divorcing. Does this mean I should dismiss my divorce?

Strong feelings of caring about your spouse often persist after a divorce is filed. Whether or not to proceed with a divorce is a deeply personal decision. Although feelings can inform us of our thoughts, feelings can also cause us not to look clearly at everything there is to see in our situation.

Have you and your spouse participated in marriage counseling? Has your spouse refused to seek treatment for an addiction? Are you worried about the safety of you or your children if you remain in the marriage? Can you envision yourself as financially secure if you remain in this marriage? Is your spouse involved in another relationship?

The answers to these questions can help you get clear about whether to consider reconciliation. Talk to your attorney, therapist, or spiritual advisor to help determine the right path for you. Successful long-term reconciliations, after the divorce has been filed, are uncommon.

2.12 Will my attorney charge me for the time I spend talking about my feelings about my spouse and my divorce?

It depends. If you are paying your attorney by the hour, expect to be charged for the time your attorney spends talking with you. If your attorney is being paid a flat rate for handling your divorce, the time spent talking with you will be included in the fee. Most attorneys charge an hourly rate.

2.13 My attorney doesn't seem to realize how difficult my divorce is for me. How can I get him to understand?

Everyone wants support and compassion from the professionals who help during a divorce. Speak frankly with your attorney about your concerns. It may be that your attorney does not see your concerns as being relevant to the job of getting your desired outcome in the divorce. Your willingness to improve the communication will help your attorney understand how best to support you in the process and will help you understand which matters are best left for discussion with your therapist or a supportive friend.

2.14 I've been told not to speak ill of my spouse in front of my child, but I know she's doing this all the time. Why can't I just speak the truth?

It can be devastating for your child to hear you bad-mouthing his or her other parent. What your child needs is permission to love both of you, regardless of any bad parental behavior. The best way to support your child during this time is to encourage a positive relationship with the other parent.

2.15 Nobody in our family has ever been divorced and I feel really ashamed. Will my children feel the same way?

Making a change in how you see your family identity is huge for you. The best way to help your children is to establish a sense of pride in their new family and to look forward to the future with a real sense of possibility. Your children will have an opportunity to witness you overcoming obstacles, demonstrating independence, and moving forward in your life notwithstanding challenges. You can be a great teacher to them during this time by demonstrating pride in your family and in yourself.

2.16 I am very worried about having my deposition taken. My spouse's attorney is very aggressive, and I'm afraid I'm going to say something that will hurt my case.

A *deposition* is an opportunity for your spouse's attorney to gather information and to assess the type of witness you will be if the case proceeds to trial. Feeling anxious about your deposition is normal. However, regardless of the personality of the attorneys, most depositions in divorces are quite uneventful.

Remember, your attorney will be seated by your side at all times to support you. Ask to meet with your attorney in advance to prepare for the deposition. If you are worried about certain questions that may be asked, talk to your attorney about them. Think of it as an opportunity, and enlist your attorney's support in being well prepared. This will bring you a sense of calm.

2.17 I am still so angry at my spouse. How can I be expected to sit in the same room during a settlement conference or mediation?

If you are still very angry at your spouse, it may be beneficial to postpone the conference. You might also consider seeking counseling to support you with coping with these feelings of anger. Discuss these feelings with your attorney. He or she should be able to set up the mediation so contact between the spouses is minimized.

While mediation styles may vary, most mediation sessions do not involve the spouses sitting in the same room. This type of mediation has "shuttle" negotiations. With this method, you and your attorney remain in one room while your spouse and his or her attorney are in another. Settlement offers are then relayed between the attorneys by the mediator or facilitator.

2.18 I'm afraid I can't make it through court without having an emotional breakdown. How do I prepare?

A divorce trial can be a highly emotional time, calling for a lot of support. Some of these ideas may help you through the process:

- Meet with your attorney or the firm's support staff in advance of your court date to prepare you for court.

- Ask you attorney whether there are any documents you should review in preparation for court, such as your deposition.

- Visit the courtroom in advance to get comfortable with the surroundings.

- Ask your attorney about having a support person with you on your court date.

- Ask yourself what is the worst thing that could happen and consider what options you would have if it did.

- Avoid alcohol, eat healthy, exercise, and get plenty of rest during the period of time leading up to the court date. Each of these will help you to prepare for the emotions of the day.

- Plan what you intend to wear in advance. Small preparations will lower your stress.

- Visualize the experience going well. Picture yourself sitting in the witness chair, giving clear, confident, and truthful answers to easy questions.

- Arrive early to the courthouse and make sure you have a plan for parking your car if you are not familiar with the area.

- Take slow, deep breaths. Breathing deeply will steady your voice, calm your nerves, and improve your focus.

Finally, remember that your judge is used to seeing spouses become emotional during a divorce. Your judge will understand if this happens to you, and it will not hurt your case. Your attorney will also be prepared to support you throughout the proceedings.

2.19   I am really confused. One day I think the divorce is a mistake. The next day I know I can't go back. A few minutes later I can hardly wait to be single again. Some days I just don't believe I'm getting divorced. What's happening?

Denial, transition, and acceptance are common passages for a person going through a divorce. One moment you might feel excited about your future and a few hours later you think your life is ruined. It is helpful to remember you may not pass from one stage to the next in a direct line. Feelings of anger or sadness may rise up long after you thought you had moved on. Similarly, your mood might feel bright one day as you think about your future plans, even though you still miss your spouse.

Coping with Stress during the Divorce Process

Taking good care of yourself is essential during this period of your life. What you are going through requires a tremendous amount of energy. Allow yourself to experience your emotions, but also continue to move forward with your life. These steps will help your life get easier day by day.

3

Working with Your Attorney

There is one thing you can be sure of in your divorce: you will be given plenty of advice. Well-intentioned neighbors, cousins, and even complete strangers will be happy to tell you war stories about an ex-spouse or about a sister who got divorced in Canada. Many will insist they know what you should do, even though they know nothing about the facts of your case or the law in Washington.

However, there is one person whose advice will matter to you: your attorney. Your attorney should be your trusted and supportive advocate at all times throughout your divorce. The counsel of your attorney can affect your life for years to come. You will never regret taking the time and effort to choose the right one for you.

See your relationship with your attorney as a partnership for pursuing what is most important to you. With clear and open attorney-client communication, you will have the best outcome possible and your entire divorce will be less stressful. By working closely with the right attorney, you can trust the professional advice you receive and simply thank your cousin Millie for sharing.

3.1 Where do I begin looking for an attorney for my divorce?

There are many ways to find a good divorce attorney. You can ask people you trust such as friends and family members who have gone through a divorce. Ask if they thought they had a good attorney, or if their former spouse did!

The best recommendations come from professionals who have personal knowledge of an attorney's experience and reputation. Referrals from court personnel, other attorneys, mediators, and others with a legal background are often of the highest quality. Financial advisors or accountants can be a great referral source. Many family counselors can provide good insight on who are the best family law attorneys.

Find a law firm that handles divorces as a regular part of its law practice. Firms that practice exclusively in the area of family law are highly desirable. Go online. Many attorneys have websites that provide information on their practices areas, professional associations, experience, and philosophy.

3.2   How do I know if I am choosing the right attorney?

Choosing the right attorney for your divorce is an important decision. Your attorney should be a trusted professional with whom you feel comfortable sharing information openly. He or she should be a person you can trust and who is a zealous advocate for your interests. You will rely upon your attorney to help you make many decisions throughout the course of your divorce. You will also entrust your legal counsel to make a range of strategic and procedural decisions on your behalf.

A consultation for a divorce might be your first meeting with an attorney. Know that attorneys want to be supportive and to fully inform you. Feel free to seek all of the information you need to help you feel secure in knowing you have made the right choice.

Find an attorney who practices primarily in the family law area. This cannot be stressed enough. Although many attorneys handle divorces, it is likely you will have more effective representation at a lower cost from an attorney who already knows the fundamentals of divorce law in Washington.

Determine the level of experience you desire in your attorney. For example, if you have had a short marriage, have few assets, and/or have no child-related issues, an attorney with less experience might be a good value for your legal needs. However, if you are anticipating a custody dispute or have complex or substantial assets, a more experienced attorney may better meet your needs. If you have issues such as business valuations or professional practices, this requires you to be even more selective. Only a small percentage of divorce attorneys have extensive experience in business and professional practice valuation.

It is important that you feel confident in the attorney you hire. If you are unsure about whether the attorney is really listening to you or understanding your concerns, keep looking until you find one who does. Your divorce is an important matter. It is critical you have a professional you can trust.

3.3   Should I hire a "bulldog"—a very aggressive attorney?

Again, consider the qualities in an attorney that are important to you. A "bulldog" may promise to be overly aggressive and take your spouse for everything he or she is worth. However, the most experienced, professional, and effective attorneys rarely make such claims or boasts. A quality attorney knows when to be aggressive but also when it is time to settle. Be careful of attorneys who appear less than professional. The judge is not swayed by boasts and false bravado. The judge will rule in favor of the party who is well prepared, offers the most compelling evidence, and whose attorney is skilled in making a legal argument.

Additionally, expect the cost of your divorce to exponentially increase if your attorney is unwilling to negotiate and drags your spouse into court at every opportunity. Look for an attorney who can represent you with zealous advocacy, while at the same time maintaining a high level of courtesy, professionalism, and integrity.

3.4   Should I interview more than one attorney?

Not necessarily. Whether you interview more than one attorney depends on the strength of your referral. If, for example, an attorney, accountant, or other trusted associate refers you to an experienced divorce attorney, you can probably be quite confident about that referral. If you have done your research and you feel confident about the attorney during your initial consultation, it may be wise to hire the attorney at that time.

However, if you did not receive a strong referral or if you don't feel confident during the initial consultation, be willing to interview more than one attorney. Every attorney has different strengths, and it is important to find the right attorney for you.

Sometimes, it is only by meeting with more than one attorney that you see clearly who will best be able to help you reach your goals in the way you want.

A word of caution is in order. The demand is high for the most experienced and successful divorce attorneys. It is not unusual for these attorneys to turn down twenty cases for each one they accept. These attorneys keep a carefully managed caseload. Once their caseload limit is met, they will not accept other cases. If you meet with such an attorney and delay in hiring him or her, you may very well lose the opportunity to retain that attorney altogether. It is wise to invest effort at the outset in making the right choice.

3.5 My spouse says that since we're still friends, we should use the same attorney for the divorce. Is this a good idea?

No. In Washington, the *Rules of Professional Conduct (RPC)* prohibit a divorce attorney from representing both spouses. There is good reason for this rule. Even the most amicable of divorcing couples usually have differing interests. It is practically impossible for an attorney to give one spouse good advice (for example how to limit spousal maintenance), without impairing the rights of the other party.

Sometimes couples have reached agreements without understanding all of their rights under the law. Many clients do not know, for example, that Washington allows a party to ask the court to order post secondary (college) support for their children. There are other issues that are not even obvious to attorneys who do not regularly practice in the area of family law. A client often will benefit from receiving further legal advice on matters such as tax considerations, retirement, and health insurance issues.

It is not uncommon for one party to retain an attorney and for the other party not to do so. In such cases, the party with the attorney files the petition for dissolution, and agreements reached between the parties are typically sent to the spouse for approval prior to any court hearing. If your spouse has filed for divorce and has said you do not need an attorney, you should nevertheless meet with an attorney for advice on how to proceed. Proceeding without an attorney could affect your legal rights, and many spouses have been taken advantage of by the spouse who has an attorney. I have seen cases where the losses were extremely significant, and by the time the unrepresented spouse realized they had been taken advantage of, the losses could not be remedied as the final divorce decree had been entered too far in the past.

3.6 What information should I take with me to the first meeting with an attorney?

Attorneys differ on the amount of information they like to see at an initial consultation. If a court proceeding, either a divorce or a protection order, has already been initiated by either you or your spouse, it is important to take copies of any court documents.

If you have a *prenuptial* or *postnuptial agreement,* a written agreement that directs how matters will be handled in the event of a divorce, with your spouse, that is another important document for you to bring at the outset of your case.

If you intend to ask for support, either for yourself or for your children, documents evidencing income of both you and your spouse will also be useful. These might include:

- Recent pay stubs
- Three years of individual and business tax returns, W-2s, and 1099s
- Bank statements showing deposits
- A statement of your monthly budget

Your attorney will also cover these areas with you at the time of your first meeting. Thus, if your situation is urgent or you do not have access to these documents, do not let it stop you from scheduling your appointment with an attorney. In the beginning, prompt legal advice about your rights is often more important than having detailed financial information. Your attorney can explain to you the options for obtaining these financial records if they are not readily available to you and you can get these documents at a later date without harming your case.

3.7 What unfamiliar words might an attorney use at the first meeting?

Law has a language all its own, and attorneys sometimes lapse into "legalese," forgetting non-attorneys may not recognize words used daily in the practice of law. Some words and phrases you might hear include:

- *Dissolution of marriage*—The divorce
- *Petitioner*—Person who files the divorce petition
- *Respondent*—Person who did not file the divorce petition
- *Jurisdiction*—Authority of a court to make rulings affecting a party
- *Service*—Process of notifying a party about a legal filing
- *Discovery*—Process during which each side provides information to each other
- *Decree*—The final order entered in a divorce

Never hesitate to ask your attorney the meaning of a term. Your complete understanding of your attorney's advice is essential for you to partner with your advocate as effectively as possible.

3.8 What can I expect at an initial consultation with an attorney?

Most attorneys will ask a comprehensive set of questions about your case. Some questions may be trivial, but may be necessary to complete initial documents, such as the Vital Statistics and Confidential Information forms. With few exceptions, attorneys are required to keep confidential all information provided. The nature of the advice you get from an attorney in an initial consultation will depend upon whether you are still deciding if you want a divorce, if you are planning for a possible divorce in the future, or if you are ready to file for divorce right away.

During the meeting, you will have an opportunity to provide the following information to the attorney:

- A brief history of your marriage

- Background information regarding yourself, your spouse, and your children
- Your immediate situation
- Your intentions and goals regarding your relationship with your spouse
- What information you are seeking from the attorney during the consultation

You can expect the attorney to provide the following information to you:

- The procedure for divorce in Washington
- The issues important in your case
- A preliminary assessment of your rights and responsibilities under the law
- Background information regarding the firm
- Information about fees and filings

Although some questions may be difficult or impossible for the attorney to answer at the initial consultation because additional information or research is needed, the initial consultation is an opportunity for you to ask all of your questions. You should leave the consultation with a much better understanding of your case.

3.9   Will the communication with my attorney be confidential?

Yes. Your attorney has an ethical duty to maintain your confidentiality. This duty of confidentiality extends to the legal staff working with your attorney. The privileged information you share with your attorney will remain private and confidential, unless such privilege is waived by your voluntarily disclosing it to third parties.

3.10   Is there any way I could inadvertently waive the attorney-client privilege as it relates to the duty of confidentiality?

Yes. To ensure that communications between you and your attorney remain confidential, and to protect against the voluntary or involuntary waiver of such privilege, below are some tips to consider:

- Refrain from disclosing the content of the communications with your attorney, or discussing in substantive detail the communications with your attorney, with third parties. Third parties include friends and family members.

- Social media provides the potential for waiving the attorney-client privilege by your publicly disclosing confidential information. Do not post information or send messages relating to your case on Facebook, Twitter, or other social media websites.

- Do not post information relating to your case or communications with your attorney on a personal blog, video blog, online chat rooms, or online message boards.

- Do not use your work-related e-mail to communicate with your attorney, or to discuss your case.

- Depending upon your employer's policy regarding electronic communication, the attorney-client privilege may be waived by communicating with your attorney or by discussing your case through your personal e-mail account (Gmail, Yahoo, etc.) via a company computer. To ensure your communications remain confidential, it is best to only communicate via e-mail from your private e-mail address from your home computer.

3.11 Can I take a friend or family member to my initial consultation?

Yes, but only if you feel doing so is truly necessary. Having someone present during your initial consultation can be a source of great support, and if you feel uncomfortable in going alone, there is nothing wrong with this support. However, it is generally more efficient if you arrive alone so your attorney can focus his or her time and attention on you. Remember, this is your consultation, and it is important the attorney hears the facts of your case directly from you. Also, be sure to ask your attorney how having a third party present at your consultation could impact the attorney-client privilege.

3.12 What exactly will my attorney do to help me get a divorce?

Your attorney will play a critical role in helping to resolve your divorce. You will be actively involved in some of the work, but other actions will be taken behind the scenes at the law office, a law library, or the courthouse.

Your attorney may perform any of the following tasks on your behalf:

- Assess the case to determine which court has jurisdiction to hear your divorce
- Develop a strategy for advising you about all aspects of your divorce, including the treatment of assets and matters concerning children
- Prepare legal documents for filing with the court
- Conduct discovery to obtain information from the other party, which could include depositions, requests for production of documents, and written interrogatories
- Appear with you at all court appearances, depositions, and conferences.
- Schedule all deadlines and court appearances
- Support you in responding to information requests from your spouse
- Inform you of actions you are required to take
- Perform financial analyses of your case
- Conduct legal research
- Prepare you for court appearances and depositions
- Prepare your case for hearings and trial, including preparing exhibits and interviewing witnesses
- Advise you regarding your rights under the law
- Counsel you regarding the risks and benefits of negotiated settlement as compared to proceeding to trial

As your advocate, your attorney is entrusted to take all steps necessary to represent your interests in the divorce.

3.13 What professionals should I expect to work with during my divorce?

Depending upon the issues identified by your attorney, you can expect to work with various types of professionals, such as appraisers, financial professionals, real estate agents, and mental health experts.

Additionally, in some cases where custody or parenting time issues are seriously disputed, the court may appoint a *guardian ad litem (GAL)*. This person, usually an attorney, has the duty to represent the best interests of the child. A guardian *ad litem* has the responsibility to investigate you and your spouse as well as the needs of your child. She or he may then be called as a witness at trial to testify regarding any relevant observations.

Another expert who could be appointed by the court is a psychologist. The role of the psychologist will depend upon the purpose for which she or he was appointed. For example, the psychologist may be appointed to perform a child-custody evaluation, which involves assessing both parents and the child, or this expert may be ordered to evaluate one parent to assess the child's safety while spending time with that parent.

3.14 I've been divorced before and I don't think I need an attorney this time. However, my spouse is hiring one. Is it wise to go it alone?

Having gone through a prior divorce, it is likely you have learned a great deal about the divorce process and your legal rights. However, there are many reasons to be extremely cautious about proceeding without legal representation. It is important to remember that every divorce is different. The length of the marriage, whether there are children, the relative financial situation for you and your spouse, as well as your age and health can all affect the financial outcome in your divorce.

Further, the law may have changed since your last divorce. Some aspects of divorce law are likely to change each year. New laws are passed and new decisions are handed down by the Washington Supreme Court and the Washington Court of Appeals which affect the rights and responsibilities of people who divorce. Some of these changes can be very substantial.

One of the most overlooked reasons why counsel is needed is that the assigned judge is likely different than in your prior divorce. Unless you live in a small county with only one or two judges, the likelihood of being assigned the same judge is low. Each judge has certain preferences, and only experienced family law counsel knows those preferences. What may have been an effective presentation with one judge may fail with another.

At a minimum, have an initial consultation with an attorney to discuss your rights. Discuss how this divorce may be different from your prior divorce. Always have an attorney review any final agreement.

3.15   Can I bring my children to meetings with my attorney?

It is best to make other arrangements for your children when you meet with your attorney. Your attorney will be giving you a great deal of important information during your conferences, and it is necessary to give him or her your full attention. Children can be distracting to both you and your attorney.

It is also recommended that you take every measure to keep information about the legal aspects of your divorce away from your children. Knowledge that you are seeing an attorney can add to your child's anxiety about the process. It can also make your child a target for questioning by the other parent about your contacts with your attorney. Judges typically take a very dim view on exposing your children to the attorneys and to the litigation process.

Most law offices are not designed to accommodate young children and ordinarily are not "childproof." For both your child's well-being and your own peace of mind, explore options for someone to care for your child when you meet with your attorney. On a similar note, never bring your children to court with you. Such conduct may bring a swift rebuke from the judge.

3.16   What is the role of the *paralegal* or *legal assistant* in my attorney's office?

A *paralegal,* or *legal assistant,* is a trained legal professional whose duties include providing support for you and your attorney. Working with a paralegal can make your divorce easier because he or she is likely to be very available to help you. It can also lower your legal costs, as the hourly rate for paralegal services is less than the rate for attorneys.

A paralegal is prohibited from giving legal advice. It is important to respect the limits of the paralegal's role if he or she is unable to answer your question because it calls for giving a legal opinion. However, a paralegal can help by receiving information from you, reviewing documents with you, providing updates of your case, and answering questions about the divorce process that do not call for legal advice.

3.17 My attorney is not returning my phone calls. What can I do?

You have a right to expect your phone calls to be returned by your attorney. Here are some options to consider:

- Ask to speak to the paralegal or another attorney in the office.

- Send an e-mail or fax telling your attorney that you have been trying to reach him or her by phone and explaining the reason it is important that you receive a call.

- Ask the receptionist to schedule a phone conference for you to speak with your attorney at a specific date and time.

- Schedule a meeting with your attorney to discuss both the issue needing attention as well as your concerns about the communication.

Your attorney wants to provide good service to you. If your calls are not being returned, take action to get the communication with your attorney back on track.

3.18 How do I know when it's time to change attorneys?

Changing attorneys is costly. You will incur legal fees for your new attorney to review information that is already familiar to your current attorney. You will spend time giving much of the same information to your new attorney that you gave to the one you have discharged. Further, a change in attorneys often results in delays in the divorce. Accordingly, a decision to change attorneys is one that you should make carefully.

The following are questions to ask yourself when you're deciding whether to stay with your attorney or seek new counsel:

- Have I spoken directly to my attorney about my concerns?
- When I expressed concerns, did my attorney take action accordingly?
- Is my attorney open and receptive to what I have to say?
- Am I blaming my attorney for the bad behavior of my spouse or opposing counsel?
- Have I provided my attorney the information needed for taking the next action?
- Does my attorney have control over the complaints I have, or are they ruled by the law or the judge?
- Is my attorney keeping promises for completing actions in my case?
- Do I trust my attorney?

Every effort should be made to resolve concerns with your attorney. If you have made this effort and the situation remains unchanged, it *may* be time to switch attorneys. However, there are times that you *should* change your attorney. The following are examples of circumstances that would indicate you should give strong consideration to immediately changing attorneys:

- Your attorney does not show up for your court hearing without a very good reason, or is late for multiple hearings
- Your attorney's courtroom performance is substantially inferior to the other attorney's performance and you get a poor ruling from the judge as a result
- Your attorney's written work product is consistently inferior to the other attorney's written work product
- Your attorney does not provide you with regular billing statements (usually monthly) after requests by you for such statements

3.19 Are there certain expectations that I should have when working with my legal team?

Yes, your legal team will be able to provide you with support and guidance during this process. There are certain actions you can expect your legal team to do for you during your divorce. The following includes actions to expect.

Meet with you prior to the filing of a court action to advise you on actions you should take first. There may be important steps to take before you initiate the legal process. Your legal team can support you to be well prepared prior to initiating divorce.

Provide a high-quality work product. Declarations and affidavits should be obtained and drafted by your attorney, not by you, the client. Handwritten statements should never be used. Documents should be of professional appearance and free of errors.

Take action to obtain a temporary court order or to enforce existing orders. Temporary court orders are often needed to ensure clarity regarding rights and responsibilities while your divorce is pending. Your legal team can help you obtain a temporary order and ask the court to enforce its order if there is a violation.

Explain the legal process during each step of your case. Understanding the legal process reduces the stress of your divorce. Your legal team can guide you each step of the way.

Listen to your concerns and answer any questions. Although only the attorneys can give you legal advice, everyone on your team is available to listen, to provide support, and to direct you to the right person who can help.

Support you in developing your parenting plan. Many parents do not know how to decide what type of parenting plan is best for their children. Your legal team can help you look at the needs of your children and offer advice based on their experience in working with families.

Support you in the completion of your discovery responses and preparing for depositions. The "discovery" process can be overwhelming for anyone. You will be asked to provide many documents with detailed information. Your legal team can make this job easier. Just ask. If your case involves depositions, your legal team will support you to be fully prepared for the experience.

Identify important issues, analyze the evidence, and advise you. Divorce is complex. Often there is a great deal of uncertainty. Your legal team can analyze the unique facts of your case and advise you based upon the law and their expertise.

Communicate with the opposing party's attorney to try to resolve issues without going to court, and to keep your case progressing. Although your attorney cannot control the actions of the opposing party or their attorney, your attorney can always initiate communication as your advocate. Phoning, e-mailing, or writing to opposing counsel are actions your legal team can take to encourage cooperation and to keep your divorce moving forward at the pace you want without the expense of contested litigation.

Think creatively regarding challenges with your case and provide options for your consideration. At the outset, you may see many obstacles to reaching a final resolution. Your legal team can offer creative ideas for resolving challenges and help you to explore your options to achieve the best possible outcome.

Facilitate the settlement process. Although your legal team can never make the other party settle, your attorney can take action to promote settlement. They can prepare settlement proposals, invite settlement conferences, and negotiate zealously on your behalf.

3.20 Are there certain things my legal team will not be able to do?

Yes. Although there are many ways in which your legal team can support you during your divorce, there are also things your legal team will not be able to accomplish, such as:

Force the other parent to exercise their parenting time. Your legal team cannot force a parent to exercise parenting time. However, be mindful that a chronic neglect of parenting time may be a basis for modifying your parenting plan. Tell your attorney if the other parent is repeatedly failing to exercise their parenting time.

Force the other party to respond to a settlement proposal. Your attorney may send proposals or make requests to opposing counsel; however, there is no duty to respond. After repeated follow-ups without a response, it may be clear no response is coming. At that time, your attorney will decide whether the issues merit court action. Both parties must agree on all terms for a case to be settled without a trial. If one party wants to proceed to trial, even over a single issue, he or she will be able to do so.

Control the tone of communication from opposing counsel or communications from the other party, or the other party's family members. Unfortunately, communication from the opposing attorney may sometimes appear rude, condescending, or demanding. Your legal team cannot stop an attorney from using these tactics.

Absent a pattern of harassment, your legal team cannot stop the other party or third parties from contacting you. If you do not want the contact, talk with your attorney about how to best handle the situation. Of course, appropriate communication regarding your children is always encouraged.

Ask the court to compensate you for every wrong done to you by the other party over the course of your marriage. Although your attorney will empathize that you do have valid complaints, please understand that focusing on the most important issues will yield the best outcome in the end. Raising numerous small issues may distract from your most important goals.

Remedy poor financial decisions made during the marriage. With few exceptions, the court's duty is to divide the marital estate as it currently exists. The judge will not attempt to remedy all past financial wrongs, such as overspending or poor investments by your spouse. If there is significant debt, consult with your attorney. Your attorney may recommend a debt counselor or bankruptcy attorney.

Control how the other party parents your children during his or her parenting time. Each parent has strengths and weaknesses. Absent special needs of a child, most judges will not issue orders regarding bedtimes, amount of television watched, playing video games, discipline methods, clothing, or diet. Of course, any suspected abuse should be reported immediately to the appropriate authorities and to your attorney.

Demand an accounting of how a parent uses court-ordered child support. Absent extraordinary circumstances, the court will generally not order the other parent to provide an accounting for the use of child support.

Leverage money for rights regarding your children. Tactics oriented toward asserting custody rights as leverage toward attaining financial goals will be discouraged. Your legal team should negotiate parenting issues based solely on considerations related to your child, and then separately negotiate child support based on financial considerations.

Guarantee payment of child support and/or spousal maintenance. Enforcement of payment of support is only possible when it is court ordered. However, even with a court order, you may experience inconsistent timing of payments due to job loss or a refusal to pay. Talk with your attorney if a pattern of repeated missed payments has developed.

Collect child care and uninsured medical expenses if provisions of the decree are not complied with. If your decree requires you to provide documentation of payment of expenses to the other party and you fail to, you could be prohibited from collecting reimbursement for those expenses. Follow the court's orders on providing documentation to the other parent, even if they do not pay as they should. Always keep records of these expenses and payments, and keep copies of communications with the other parent regarding payment or reimbursement. It is much easier to keep these records on an ongoing basis than to get copies of old checks, day care bills, medical bills, and insurance documents at a later time.

4

Attorney Fees and Costs

Anytime you make a major investment, you want to know what the cost is going to be and what you are getting for your money. Investing in quality legal representation for your divorce is no different. The cost of your divorce might be one of your greatest concerns. Because of this, you will want to be an intelligent consumer of legal services. You want quality, but you also want to get the best value for the fees you are paying.

Legal fees for a divorce can be costly and the total expense is not always predictable. However, there are many actions you can take to estimate and control the cost. Develop a plan early for how you will finance your divorce. Speak openly with your attorney about fees from the outset. Learn as much as you can about how you will be charged. Insist on a written fee agreement. By being informed, aware, and wise, your financial investment in your divorce will be money well spent in protecting your future.

4.1 Can I get free legal advice from an attorney over the phone?

Every law firm has its own policy regarding attorneys talking to people who are not yet clients of the firm. Most questions about your divorce are too complex for an attorney to give a meaningful answer during a brief phone call. Questions about your divorce require a complete look at the facts, circumstances, and background of your marriage. To obtain good legal advice, it is best to schedule an initial consultation with an attorney whose practice focuses on divorce and family law. Rarely will you get quality, reliable legal advice over the phone from an attorney you have not yet retained.

4.2 Will I be charged for an initial consultation with an attorney?

It depends. Some attorneys give free consultations, while others charge a fee. When scheduling your appointment, you should be told the amount of the fee. Payment is ordinarily due at the time of the consultation. It is important to understand that the most experienced and successful family law attorneys are highly sought after. Because of the demand for their services, they turn away many cases for each case they agree to work on. Such attorneys are generally not going to offer a free initial consultation. However, it is entirely possible a qualified attorney with less experience is willing to offer a free consultation and might be a very good selection for your representation depending on your particular budget.

4.3 If I decide to hire an attorney, when do I have to pay him or her?

If your attorney charges for an initial consultation, be prepared to make payment at the time of your meeting. At the close of your consultation, the attorney will tell you if they are willing to accept your case. If they are willing to accept your case, the attorney will tell you the amount of the retainer. In many cases, the attorney will inform you of the firm's retainer requirements during your initial phone conference when you are setting up the initial consultation. This will help you determine if this firm will fit into your budgetary constraints.

If you are not comfortable with your attorney during the initial consultation, or desire to interview other attorneys, you are not required to pay a retainer. Keep in mind that if you choose not to hire an experienced attorney at the time of your initial consultation, the attorney may not have another opening if you decide to hire him or her at a later date. If you think you might want to hire this attorney, it is always a good idea to be prepared to do so at the initial consultation.

4.4 What exactly is a *retainer* and how much can I expect mine to be?

A *retainer* is a sum paid to your attorney in advance for services to be performed and costs to be incurred in your divorce. This will be either an amount paid toward a "flat fee" for your divorce, or an advance credit for services that will be charged by the hour. If your case is accepted by the law firm, expect the attorney to request a retainer following the initial consultation.

Retainers vary depending on the issues presented by your particular divorce. Child-custody matters, business valuation cases, significant-asset cases, and interstate parenting disputes often have higher retainers due to the costs involved.

The amount of retainer can also vary with the county you are filing in. Attorneys in King, Pierce, Spokane, and other populous counties are likely to charge a higher retainer due to demand and overhead costs. Clarify with your attorney at the outset what the charges will be and how you will be charged.

A word of warning is warranted. A lower retainer is not necessarily a better bargain. A retainer simply assures an attorney that you have sufficient funds to pay your bill and pay for costs such as appraisals, filing fees, and service fees. Quality, experienced attorneys usually charge a higher retainer because the demand for their services allows them to do so. Less experienced attorneys or those less successful are often forced to lower their retainer to attract clients.

However, the experienced attorney knows what needs to be done and can often do it quicker and with better quality than less experienced counsel. Accordingly, by the end of your case, the most experienced and successful attorneys often end up costing the same *or less* than their less experienced colleagues. The old adage is usually true: You get what you pay for. A divorce can be life altering. Get the best counsel that you can reasonably afford.

4.5 Will my attorney accept my divorce case on a contingency fee basis?

No. A contingency fee is an attorney fee that only becomes payable if your case is successfully resolved so that you receive some kind of monetary payment. In Washington, attorneys are prohibited from entering into a contingency fee contract in any divorce case. Your attorney may not accept payment based upon securing your divorce, the amount of spousal maintenance or support awarded, or the division of the property settlement.

4.6   How much does it cost to get a divorce?

The cost of your divorce will depend upon many factors. Some attorneys charge a *flat fee*. This is a fixed amount for the legal services being provided. A flat fee is more likely to be used when there are no children of the marriage and the parties have agreed upon the division of their property and debts. Usually, these are simple, uncontested cases. However, most Washington attorneys charge by the hour for divorces.

It is important that you discuss the cost of your divorce at your first meeting with your attorney. As previously discussed, it is customary for family law attorneys to request a retainer, also known as a *fee advance,* prior to beginning work on your case. Be sure to ask your attorney what portion, if any, of the retainer is refundable if you do not continue with the case or if you terminate your relationship with the attorney. With some exceptions, Washington generally requires that the retainer be refundable to the extent not actually earned.

If your case is not contested, but still settles relatively quickly, it is not uncommon for total fees to run in the $2,000.00 to $4,000.00 range. Cases that have more extensive litigation but settle before a trial can often be completed for less than $10,000.00. Cases that have a very high level of litigation, that have substantial assets that must be valued, or that go to trial, will likely exceed $10,000.00. Again, these are very general estimates. Talk with your attorney about what she or he estimates your possible total fee to be.

4.7   What are typical hourly rates for a divorce attorney?

Washington is a very diverse state. In some areas of the state there is increased overhead and it is very expensive to practice, so attorney fees are higher. For example, attorney hourly rates in King County will often be substantially higher than in smaller outlying counties. Attorney hourly rates in Spokane County will typically be higher than those found in outlying counties in that geographic area, but still substantially less than in King County. King County hourly rates can be $350.00 per hour or even higher. Spokane County hourly rates can be $250.00 per hour. Again, rates vary substantially throughout the state, with the most experienced and successful attorneys usually charging the higher rates for that particular county.

The rate your attorney charges may also depend upon factors such as skills, reputation, exclusive focus on divorce law, and what other attorneys in the area are charging. Sometimes, attorneys with ten years of experience are more skilled and successful than attorneys with thirty years of experience. This is another reason why it is important to get a quality referral.

If you have a concern about the amount of an attorney's hourly rate, the amount of the retainer, or if the senior attorney is not accepting cases, but you would like to hire the firm with which the attorney is associated, consider asking to work with an *associate attorney* in the firm. Associates are attorneys who ordinarily have less experience than the senior partners. However, they often are extensively trained and mentored by the senior partners, are very experienced, and are fully capable of handling your case.

4.8   If I can't afford to pay the full amount of the retainer, can I make monthly payments to my attorney?

Every law firm has its own policy regarding payment arrangements for divorce clients. Often, these arrangements are tailored to the specific client. Most attorneys will require a substantial retainer to be paid at the outset of your case. Some attorneys may accept monthly payments in lieu of the retainer, but this is far less likely with experienced, in-demand counsel. Most will require monthly payments in addition to the initial retainer, or request additional retainers as your case progresses. Ask frank questions of your attorney to have clarity about your responsibility for payment of legal fees. The attorney should also set forth his or her billing practices and payment expectations in the written fee agreement that you should be provided at the outset of representation.

4.9 I agreed to pay my attorney a substantial retainer to begin my case. Will I still have to make monthly payments?

Ask your attorney what will be expected of you regarding payments on your account while the divorce is in progress. Understand whether monthly payments on your account will be expected, whether it is likely that you will be asked to pay additional retainers, and whether the firm charges interest on past due accounts. Regular payments to your attorney can help you avoid having a burdensome legal bill at the end of your case. Additionally, you may also be required to keep a minimum credit balance in your account to ensure your case is adequately funded for ongoing work by your legal team.

4.10 My attorney gave me an estimate of the cost of my divorce and it sounds reasonable. Do I still need a written fee agreement?

Absolutely. Insist upon a written agreement with your attorney. It is essential not only to define the scope of the services for which you have hired your attorney, but also to ensure that you have clarity about matters such as your attorney's hourly rate, whether you will be billed for certain costs such as copying, and when you can expect to receive statements on your account. A clear fee agreement reduces the risk of misunderstandings between you and your attorney. It supports you both in being clear about your promises to one another so your focus can be on the legal services being provided rather than on disputes about your fees.

4.11 How will I know how the fees and charges are accumulating?

Be sure your written fee agreement with your attorney is clear about how you will be informed regarding the status of your account. At the outset of your case, be sure your written fee agreement includes a provision for the attorney to provide you with regular statements of your account. It is reasonable to ask these be provided monthly.

Review the statement of your account promptly after you receive it. Check to make sure there are no errors, such as duplicate billing entries. If your statement reflects work that you were unaware was performed, call for clarification. Your attorney's office should welcome any questions you have about services it provided.

Your statement may also include filing fees, court reporter fees for transcripts of court testimony or depositions, copy expenses, or interest charged on your account. If more than a month has passed and you have not received a statement on your account, call your attorney's office to request one. Legal fees can mount quickly, and it is important you stay aware of the status of your legal expenses.

4.12 What other expenses are related to the divorce litigation besides attorney fees?

Talk to your attorney about costs other than the attorney fees. Ask whether it is likely to include filing fees, service fees, court reporter expenses, expert-witness fees, appraisals or evaluations, mediation expenses, or guardian *ad litem* fees. Expert-witness fees can be a substantial expense, ranging from hundreds to thousands of dollars, depending upon the type of expert and the extent to which he or she is involved in your case. Speak frankly with your attorney about these costs so that together you can make the best decisions about how to use your budget for the litigation.

4.13 Who pays for experts such as appraisers, accountants, psychologists, and mediators?

Costs for the services of experts, whether appointed by the court or hired by the parties, are ordinarily paid for by the parties themselves. In the case of the guardian *ad litem* who may be appointed to represent the best interests of your children, the amount of the fee will depend upon how much time this professional spends. The judge often orders this fee to be shared by the parties. However, depending upon the circumstances, one party can be ordered to pay the entire fee or a majority of the fee. If you can demonstrate *indigence,* that is, a very low income and no ability to pay, the county may be ordered to pay your share of the guardian *ad litem* fee.

Psychologists either charge by the hour or set a flat fee for a certain type of evaluation. Again, the court can order one party to pay this fee or both parties to share the expense in some proportion. It is not uncommon for a psychologist to request payment in advance and hold the release of an expert report until fees are paid.

Mediators either charge a flat fee per session or an hourly rate fee. Generally, each party will pay one half of the mediator's fee, which is paid prior to your mediation sessions. If one spouse earns substantially more than the other, the spouse with more income can be ordered to pay a greater share, or all, of the mediation fees.

The fees for many experts, including appraisers and accountants, will vary depending upon whether the individuals are called upon to provide only a specific service such as an appraisal, or whether they will need to prepare for giving testimony and appear as a witness at trial. Your attorney should be able to give you an estimate of the likely fees.

4.14 What factors will impact how much my divorce will cost?

Although it is often difficult to predict how much your legal fees will be, the following are some of the factors that affect the cost:

- Whether there are children
- Whether child custody is agreed upon
- Whether there are novel legal questions
- Whether a pension plan will be divided between the parties
- The nature of the issues contested
- The number of issues agreed to by the parties
- The cooperation of the opposing party and opposing counsel
- The frequency of your communication with your legal team
- The ability of the parties to communicate with each other, as well as the client's ability to communicate with her attorney
- The promptness with which information is provided and/or exchanged between both the clients and the attorneys

- Whether there are litigation costs, such as fees for expert witnesses or court reporters
- The hourly rate of the attorney
- The time it will take to conclude your divorce

Communicating with your attorney regularly about your legal fees will help you to have a better understanding of the overall cost as your case proceeds.

4.15 Will my attorney charge for phone calls and e-mails?

You should expect to be billed for any communication with your attorney. Many professional services provided by attorneys are done via phone and e-mail. This time may be spent giving legal advice, negotiating, or gathering information to protect your interests. These calls and e-mails are all legal services for which you should anticipate being charged by your attorney.

To make the most of your time during attorney phone calls, plan your call in advance. Organize the information you want to relay, your questions, and any concerns to be addressed. This will help you to be clear and focused during the phone call so your fees are well spent.

4.16 Will I be charged for talking to the staff at my attorney's office?

It depends. Check the terms of your fee agreement with your attorney. Whether you are charged fees for talking to non-attorney members of the law office may depend upon their role in the office. For example, many law firms charge for the services of paralegals and law clerks.

Remember that non-attorneys cannot give legal advice, so it is important to respect their roles. Don't expect the receptionist to give you an opinion regarding whether you will win custody or receive spousal maintenance. Your attorney's support staff will be able to relay your messages and receive information from you. They may also be able to answer many of your questions. Allowing this type of support from within the firm is another important way to control your legal fees.

4.17   What is a *litigation estimate,* and how do I know if I need one?

If your case is complex and you are anticipating substantial legal fees, ask your attorney to prepare a *litigation estimate* for your review. This can help you understand the nature of the services anticipated, the time that may be spent, and the overall amount it will cost to proceed to trial. The litigation estimate will likely be comprised of a combination of your attorney and your legal team's hourly rates. It can also be helpful for budgeting and planning for expert-witness fees and appraisal costs. Knowing the anticipated costs of litigation can help you make meaningful decisions about which issues to litigate and which to consider resolving through settlement negotiations.

4.18   What is a *trial retainer* and will I have to pay one?

The purpose of the *trial retainer* is to fund the work needed to prepare for trial and for services required during the day or days of trial, which could include attorney fees and witness costs. A trial retainer is a sum of money paid on your account with your attorney when it appears as though your case may not settle and is at risk of proceeding to trial. It is often based upon the number of days your case is certified for trial. A trial retainer is different from an initial divorce case retainer in that it will usually not be required if your case is settled sufficiently in advance of the trial date.

Confirm with your attorney that any unearned portion of your trial retainer will be refunded if your case settles. Ask your attorney whether and when a trial retainer might be required in your case so you can avoid surprises and plan your budget accordingly. In most cases, this should be part of a written retainer agreement.

4.19   How do I know whether I should spend the attorney fees my attorney says it will require to take my case to trial?

Deciding whether to take a case to trial or to settle is often the most challenging point in the divorce process. This decision should be made with the support of your attorney. When the issues in dispute are primarily financial, often the decision about settlement is related to the costs of going to trial. Understand just how far apart you and your spouse are on the financial matters and compare this to the estimated costs of going to trial. By comparing these amounts, you can decide whether a compromise on certain financial issues is appropriate.

If your attorney is sufficiently experienced, he or she should be able to give you some prediction of what the likely range of results may be. However, no attorney can guarantee any particular result. Consult with your attorney as to whether the potential benefits of going to trial sufficiently outweigh the risks and costs associated with the trial process.

4.20   Is there any way I can reduce some of the expenses of getting a divorce?

Litigation of any kind can be expensive, and divorces are no exception. The good news is that there are many ways that you can help control the expense. Here are some ways:

Put it in writing. If you need to relay information that is important but not urgent, consider providing it to your attorney by mail, fax, or e-mail. This creates a prompt and accurate record for your file and takes less time than exchanging phone messages and talking on the phone.

Keep your attorney informed. Just as your attorney should keep you up to date on the status of your case, you need to do the same. Keep your attorney advised about any major developments in your life, such as plans to move, have someone move into your home, change in your employment status, or buy or sell significant property. During your divorce, if your contact information changes, be sure to notify your attorney.

Obtain copies of documents. An important part of litigation includes reviewing documents such as tax returns, account statements, report cards, or medical records. Your attorney will ordinarily be able to request or *subpoena* these items, but many may be readily available to you directly upon request. The more you can do yourself, the less your fees will be. Always ensure the information is presented to your attorney neatly and organized. If your attorney has to sort through items thrown into a box, your fees may be greater than if you had done nothing at all.

Consult your attorney's website. If your attorney has a website, it may be a great source of useful information. The answers to commonly asked questions about the divorce process can often be found there.

Utilize support professionals. Get to know the support staff at your attorney's office. Although only attorneys are able to give you legal advice, the receptionist, paralegal, legal secretary, or law clerk may be able to answer your questions regarding the status of your case. All communication with any professionals in a law firm is required to be kept strictly confidential.

Consider working with an associate attorney. Although the senior attorneys or partners in a law firm may have more experience, you may find that working with an associate attorney is a good option. Hourly rates for an associate attorney are sometimes lower than those charged by a senior partner and the associate may be more available to assist you, particularly if the senior partner is in a trial. Frequently, the associate attorney has trained under a senior partner and developed excellent skills as well as knowledge of the law.

Leave a detailed message. If your attorney knows the information you are seeking, she or he can often get the answer before returning your call. This not only gets your answer faster, but also reduces costs.

Discuss more than one matter during a call. It is not unusual for clients to have many questions during litigation. If your question is not urgent, consider waiting to call until you have more than one inquiry. However, never hesitate to call to ask any legal question.

Provide timely responses to information requests. Whenever possible, provide information requested by your attorney in a timely manner. This avoids the cost of follow-up action by your attorney and the additional expense of extending the time in litigation.

Carefully review your monthly statements. Scrutinize your monthly billing statements closely. If you believe an error has been made, contact your attorney's office right away to discuss your concerns. Your attorney will want to make things right.

Remain open to settlement. Understand that when your disagreement concerns financial matters, the value of money in dispute may be less than the amount it will cost to go to trial. By doing your part, you can use your legal fees wisely and control the costs of your divorce.

4.21 I don't have much money, but I need to hire a quality divorce attorney as quickly as possible. What should I do?

If you have limited funds to hire a quality attorney, consider some of these options:

- Borrow the legal fees from friends or family. Often those close to you are concerned about your future and would be pleased to support you in your goal of having your rights protected. Although this may be uncomfortable to do, remember that most people will appreciate that you trust them enough to ask for their help. If the retainer is too much money to request from a single individual, consider whether a handful of persons might each be able to contribute a lesser amount to help you reach your goal of hiring an attorney. Seeking such assistance is actually very common.

- Charge the legal fees on a low-interest credit card or consider taking out a loan. Ask a close friend and relative if you can use their credit card and pay them back when funds become available.

- Talk to your attorney about using money held in a joint account with your spouse.

- Ask your attorney about your spouse paying for your legal fees. Courts in Washington can order one spouse to pay the other spouse's attorney fees on a "need and ability to pay" basis.

- Ask your attorney about being paid from the proceeds of the property settlement. If you and your spouse have acquired substantial assets during the marriage, you may be able to find an attorney who will wait to be paid until the assets are divided at the conclusion of the divorce.

Closely examine all sources of funds readily available to you, as you may have overlooked money that might be easily accessible to you. Do not be afraid to obtain a loan. Good representation is a wise investment.

4.22 I don't have any money and I need a divorce. What are my options?

If you have a low income and few assets, you may be eligible to obtain assistance at no cost or minimal cost through one of the following organizations:

- Washington law schools frequently have legal clinics that provide divorce assistance. Call the law school closest to you and ask to speak with the law clinic.

- Call your county bar association and ask if they provide referrals for free (*pro bono*) representation or have a volunteer attorney program. Also ask for a reference to legal services organizations which may be in your county.

- Call the clerk of the Superior Court for your county and ask if it has a facilitator or other employee who helps individuals fill out divorce documents and offer other procedural advice.

These organizations have a screening process for potential clients, as well as limits on the nature of the cases they take. The demand for their services is also usually greater than the number of attorneys available to handle cases. Consequently, if you are eligible for legal services from one of these programs, you should anticipate being on a waiting list. In short, if you have very little income and few assets, you are likely to experience some delay in obtaining an attorney. If you believe you might be eligible for participation in one of these programs, inquire early to increase your opportunity to get the legal help you are seeking.

4.23 Is there anything I can do on my own to get support for my children if I don't have money for an attorney for a divorce?

Yes. If you need support for your children, contact the *Division of Child Support (DCS)* for help in obtaining a child support order. Although the DCS cannot help with matters such as custody or property division, they can pursue support from your spouse for your children. The Division of Child Support has offices throughout the state.

4.24 If my mother pays my legal fees, will my attorney give her private information about my divorce?

If someone else is paying your legal fees, discuss with your attorney and the payor your expectations that your attorney will honor the ethical duty of confidentiality. Without your permission, your attorney should not disclose information to others about your case. However, if you authorize your attorney to speak with your family members, be aware that you will be charged for these communications. Regardless of the opinions of the person who pays your attorney fees, your attorney's duty is to remain *your* zealous advocate.

4.25 Can I ask the court to order my spouse to pay my attorney fees?

Yes. If you want to ask the court to order your spouse to pay any portion of your legal fees, be sure to discuss this with your attorney at the first opportunity. Most attorneys will treat the obligation for your legal fees as yours until the other party has made payment.

If your case is likely to require costly experts and your spouse has a much greater ability to pay these expenses, talk to your attorney about the possibility of filing a motion with the court asking your spouse to pay toward these costs while the case is pending.

4.26 What happens if I don't pay my attorney the fees I promised to pay?

The ethical rules for attorneys allow your attorney to withdraw from representation if you do not comply with your fee agreement. Your attorney may also file an attorney's lien against you in order to pay any outstanding attorney fees or costs to the firm. Your fees can also be sent to collection. Consequently, it is important to keep the promises you have made regarding your account.

If you are having difficulty paying your attorney fees, talk with your attorney about payment options. Consider borrowing the funds, using your credit card, or asking for help from friends and family. Above all, do not avoid communication with your attorney if you are having challenges making payment. Keeping in touch with your attorney is essential for you to have an advocate at all stages of your divorce.

5

The Discovery Process

Discovery is one of the least talked about steps in divorce, but is often among the most important. The purpose of discovery is to ensure both you and your spouse have access to the same information. This way, you can either negotiate a fair agreement or have all of the facts and documents necessary to present to the judge at trial. The discovery process enables you and your spouse to meet on a more level playing field when it comes to settling your case or taking it to trial. You and your spouse both need the same information if you hope to reach agreement on any of the issues in your divorce. Similarly, the judge must know all of the facts to make a fair decision.

The discovery process may seem tedious at times because of the need to obtain and to provide a lot of detailed information. Completing it, however, provides clarity about the particular issues in your divorce. Trust your attorney's advice about the importance of having the necessary evidence as you complete the discovery process in order to reach your goals in your divorce.

5.1   What is the legal definition of *discovery*?

Discovery is the part of your divorce process in which the attorneys attempt to learn as much about the facts of your case as possible. Through a variety of methods, both attorneys will request information from you, your spouse, and potential witnesses in your case.

5.2 What types of discovery might be done by my attorney or my spouse's attorney?

Types of discovery include:

- Interrogatories, which are written questions that must be answered under oath
- Requests for production of documents, which asks for certain documents to be provided by you or your spouse
- Requests for admissions, which asks for certain facts to be admitted or denied
- Subpoena of documents
- Depositions in which questions are asked and answered under oath in the presence of a court reporter, but outside the presence of a judge

Factors that can influence the type of discovery conducted in your divorce can include:

- The types of issues in dispute
- How much access you and your spouse have to needed information
- The level of cooperation in sharing information
- The budget available for performing discovery

Talk to your attorney about the nature and extent of discovery anticipated in your case.

5.3 How long does the discovery process take?

Discovery can take anywhere from a few weeks to a number of months, depending upon the complexity of the case, the cooperation of you and your spouse, and whether expert witnesses are involved. The Washington Court Rules provide that interrogatories, requests for production of documents, and requests for admissions be responded to within thirty days.

5.4 My attorney insists that we conduct discovery, but I don't want to spend the time and money on it. Is it really necessary?

The discovery process can be critical to a successful outcome in your case for several reasons:

- It increases the likelihood that any agreements reached are based on accurate information
- It provides necessary information for deciding whether to settle or proceed to trial
- It supports the preparation of defenses by providing information regarding your spouse's care.
- It avoids surprises at trial, such as unexpected witness testimony.
- It ensures all potential issues are identified by your attorney.

Discuss with your attorney the intention behind the discovery being conducted in your case to ensure it is consistent with your goals and a meaningful investment of your legal fees.

5.5 I just received from my spouse's attorney interrogatories and requests that I produce documents. My attorney wants me to respond within two weeks. I'll never make the deadline. What can I do?

Answering your discovery promptly will help move your case forward and help control your legal fees. There are steps you can take to make this task easier. First, look at all of the questions. Many of them will not apply or your answers will be a simple "yes" or "no."

Ask a friend or family member to help you. It is important to develop the practice of letting others help you while you are going through your divorce. Chances are that you will make great progress in just a couple of hours with help.

Break it down into smaller tasks. If you answer a few questions a day, the task will not be so overwhelming. Also, call your attorney. Ask whether a paralegal in the office can help you organize the needed information or determine whether some of it can be provided at a later date.

Delay in the discovery process often leads to frustration by clients and attorneys. Do your best to provide the information in a timely manner with the help of others.

5.6   I don't have access to my documents and my spouse is being uncooperative in providing my attorney with information. Can my attorney request information directly from an employer or financial institution?

Yes, it may be possible to issue a subpoena directly to an employer or financial institution. A *subpoena* is a court order directing an individual or corporate representative to appear before the court or to produce documents in a pending lawsuit. In the discovery process, a subpoena is used to require an individual or corporation to produce papers, books, or other physical documents that constitute or contain evidence relevant to your case.

5.7   My spouse's attorney intends to subpoena my medical records. Aren't these private?

Whether or not your medical records are relevant will depend upon the issues in dispute. All or a portion of these records may be relevant if you are requesting spousal maintenance or if your health is an issue in the dispute of child custody. Talk with your attorney about your rights. Options are available to protect or even prevent the disclosure of your medical information, particularly information of a sensitive nature.

5.8   I own my business; will I have to disclose my business records?

Yes, you may be required to provide extensive records of your business in the discovery process. However, it is common for the court to protect the confidentiality of these records.

5.9   It's been two months since my attorney sent interrogatories to my spouse, and we still don't have his answers. I answered mine on time. Is there anything that can be done to speed up the process?

The failure or refusal of a spouse to follow the rules of discovery can add to both the frustration and expense of the divorce process. Talk with your attorney about filing a *motion to compel,* seeking a court order that your spouse must provide the requested information by a certain date. A request for attorney fees for the filing of the motion may also be appropriate. Also, ask your attorney if a subpoena of information from an employer or a financial institution is a more cost-effective way to get needed facts and documents if your spouse remains uncooperative.

5.10   What is a *deposition*?

A *deposition* is the asking and answering of questions under oath, outside of court, in the presence of a court reporter. A deposition may be taken of you, your spouse, or potential witnesses in your divorce case, including experts. Both attorneys will be present. You and your spouse also have the right to be present during the taking of depositions of any witnesses in your case. Depositions are not performed in every divorce. They are most common in cases involving contested custody, complex financial issues, and expert witnesses.

After your deposition is completed, the questions and answers will be transcribed. This means that is typed by the court reporter exactly as given and bound into one or more volumes. You will be charged a fee to obtain a copy of this transcript.

5.11   What is the purpose of a deposition?

A deposition can serve a number of purposes such as:

- Supporting the settlement process by providing valuable information
- Helping your attorney determine which witnesses to use at trial
- Aiding in the assessment of a witness's credibility, that is, whether the witness appears to be telling the truth
- Helping avoid surprises at the trial by learning the testimony of witnesses in advance
- Preserving testimony in the event the witness becomes unavailable for trial

Depositions can be essential tools in a divorce, especially when a case is likely to proceed to trial.

5.12   Will what I say in my deposition be used against me when we go to court?

Usually, a deposition is used to develop trial strategy and obtain information in preparation for trial. In some circumstances, a deposition may be used at trial. If you are called later to testify as a witness and you give testimony contrary to your deposition, your deposition can be used to impeach you by showing the inconsistency in your statements.

It is important to meet with your attorney and properly prepare for a deposition. Review any declarations you have previously filed to ensure your memory is fresh. It is also important to review your deposition prior to your live testimony to ensure consistency and to prepare yourself for the type of questions you may be asked.

5.13   Will the judge read the depositions?

Unless a witness becomes unavailable for trial or gives conflicting testimony at trial, it is unlikely that the judge will ever read the depositions. However, the judge may see the depositions when they are being used to show a witness has provided contradictory evidence previously. For these reasons, it is important to ensure your answers to deposition questions are fair and accurate.

5.14   How should I prepare for my deposition?

To prepare for your deposition, review the important documents in your case, such as the petition, your answers in discovery, your financial affidavit, and any temporary hearing affidavits. Gather all documents you have been asked to provide at your deposition. Deliver them to your attorney in advance of your deposition for copying and review. Talk with your attorney about the type of questions you can expect to be asked. Discuss with him or her any questions you are concerned about answering.

5.15   What will I be asked? Can I refuse to answer questions?

Questions in a deposition can cover a broad range of topics including your education, work, income, and family. The attorney is allowed to ask anything that is reasonably calculated to lead to the discovery of admissible evidence. This means if the question may lead to relevant information, it can be asked in a deposition, even though the information may be inadmissible later at trial. If you are unsure whether to answer a question, ask your attorney and follow his or her advice.

Your attorney may object to inappropriate questions. If there is an objection, say nothing until the attorneys discuss the objection. You will be directed whether or not to answer.

5.16   What if I give incorrect information in my deposition?

You will be under oath during your deposition, so it is very important you be truthful. If you give incorrect information by mistake, contact your attorney as soon as you realize the error. If you lie during your deposition, you risk being impeached by the other attorney during your divorce trial. This could cause you to lose credibility with the court, rendering your testimony less valuable.

5.17   What if I don't know or can't remember the answer to a question?

You may be asked questions about which you have no knowledge. It is always acceptable to say "I don't know" if you do not have the knowledge. Similarly, if you cannot remember, simply say so.

5.18   What else do I need to know about having my deposition taken?

The following suggestions will help you give a successful deposition:

- Prepare for your deposition by reviewing and providing necessary documents.
- Discuss with your attorney in advance of your deposition whether you should review the transcript of your deposition for its accuracy or whether you should waive your right to review and sign the deposition.
- Get a good night's sleep the night before. Eat a meal with protein to sustain your energy, as the length of depositions can vary.

- Arrive early for your deposition so that you have time to get comfortable with your surroundings.

- Relax. You are going to be asked questions about matters that you know. Your deposition is likely to begin with routine matters such as your education and work history.

- Tell the truth, including whether you have met with an attorney or discussed preparation for the deposition.

- Stay calm. Your spouse's attorney will be judging your credibility and demeanor. Do not argue with the attorneys.

- Listen carefully to the entire question. Do not try to anticipate questions or start thinking about your answer before the attorney has finished asking the question.

- Take your time and carefully consider the question before answering. There is no need to hurry.

- Answer the question directly. If the question calls only for "yes" or "no," provide such an answer.

- Do not volunteer information. If the attorney wants to elicit more information, he or she will do so in following questions.

- If you do not understand the question clearly, ask that it be repeated or rephrased. Do not try to answer what you *think* was asked.

- If you do not know or cannot remember the answer, say so. This is an adequate answer.

- Do not guess. If your answer is an estimate or approximation, say so. Do not let an attorney pin you down to anything you are not sure about. For example, if you cannot remember the number of times an event occurred, say that. If the attorney asks you if it was more than ten times, answer only if you can. If you can provide a range (more than ten but less than twenty) with reasonable certainty, you may do so.

- If an attorney mischaracterizes something you said earlier, say so.

- Speak clearly and loudly enough for everyone to hear you.
- Answer all questions with words, rather than gestures or sounds. "Uh-huh" is difficult for the court reporter to distinguish from "uh-uh" and may result in inaccuracies in the transcript.
- If you need a break at any point in the deposition, you have the right to request one. You can talk to your attorney during such a break.

Remember, the purpose of your deposition is to support a good outcome in your case and completing it will help move your case forward. It also gives your attorney the chance to see your strengths and weaknesses in your demeanor and delivery, and to make adjustments prior to a live hearing before a judge.

5.19 Are depositions always necessary? Does every witness have to be deposed?

Depositions are less likely to be needed if you and your spouse are reaching agreement on most of the facts in your case and you are moving toward a settlement. They are more likely to be needed in cases where child custody is disputed or where there are complex financial issues. Although depositions of all witnesses are usually unnecessary, it is common to take depositions of expert witnesses.

5.20 Will I get a copy of the depositions in my case?

Ask your attorney for copies of the depositions in your case. It will be important for you to carefully review your deposition if your case proceeds to trial. You will be charged for the deposition transcript. Typical costs are often several hundred dollars depending on the length of the deposition.

6

Mediation and Negotiation

If your marriage was full of conflict, you might be asking yourself how you can make the fighting stop. You picture your divorce as having arguing attorneys, an angry spouse, and constant litigation. You wonder if there is a way out of this never-ending conflict.

Or, perhaps you and your spouse are parting ways amicably. Although you are in disagreement about how your divorce should be settled, you are both clear that you want the process to be respectful and without hostility. You'd rather spend your hard-earned money on necessary appraisals and expert valuations.

Either way, going to trial and having a judge make the decisions in your divorce is not inevitable. In fact, most Washington cases settle without the need for a trial. Mediation and negotiation can help you and your spouse resolve your disputed issues and reach your own agreements without taking your case before a judge who will make decisions for you.

Resolving your divorce through a mediated or negotiated settlement has advantages. You can achieve a mutually satisfying agreement, a known outcome, little risk of appeal, and often enjoy significantly lower legal fees. Despite the circumstances that led to the end of your marriage, it is possible for your divorce to conclude peacefully with the help of these tools.

6.1 What is the difference between *mediation* and *negotiation*?

Both mediation and negotiation are methods used to help you and your spouse settle your divorce by reaching agreement rather than going to trial and having the judge make decisions for you. These methods are sometimes referred to as *alternative dispute resolution (ADR)*.

Mediation uses a trained mediator who is an independent, neutral third party. He or she is a skilled professional who can assist you and your spouse in the process. *Negotiation* involves attorneys for both you and your spouse. Attorneys for the spouses are usually present during mediation; their presence is highly recommended.

6.2 What is involved in the mediation process? What will I have to do and how long will it take?

The mediation process will be explained to you in detail by the mediator at the start of the mediation session. Mediation involves one or more meetings with you, your spouse, the attorneys, and the mediator. In some cases, the attorneys will be absent, but this is advisable only in cases where very little is at issue. Always talk with your attorney before proceeding to mediation unrepresented.

Prior to meeting with you and your spouse in an initial mediation session, the mediator will conduct an individual initial screening session with each of you to assess your ability to communicate with each other, and for indications of domestic abuse or other forms of intimidation or coercion. After the mediator's initial screening, he or she will decide whether you and your spouse should mediate together, or whether the mediation should take place separately. Generally, the parties work in separate rooms.

The mediator will outline ground rules designed to ensure you will be treated respectfully and given an opportunity to be heard. How long the process of mediation continues depends upon many of the same factors that affect how long your divorce will take. These include how many issues you and your spouse disagree about, the complexity of these issues, and the willingness of each of you to work toward an agreement.

Your case could settle after one mediation session or it may require a series of meetings. It is common for the mediator to clarify at the close of each session whether the parties are willing to continue with another session. It is also common for the mediator to write down the areas agreed upon and the areas that still need to be resolved.

6.3   My attorney said that mediation and negotiation can reduce delays in completing my divorce. How can they do this?

When the issues in your divorce are decided by a judge instead of by you and your spouse, there are many opportunities for delay. These can include:

- Waiting for the trial date
- Having to return to court on a later, second date if your trial is not completed on the day it is scheduled
- Waiting for the judge's ruling on your case
- Needing additional court hearings after your trial to resolve disputes about the intention of your judge's rulings, issues that were overlooked, or disagreement regarding the language of the decree

Each one of these events holds the possibility of delaying your divorce by days, weeks, or even months. Mediating or negotiating the terms of your divorce decree can eliminate these delays.

6.4   How can mediation and negotiation lower the costs of my divorce?

If your case is not settled by agreement, you will go to trial. If the issues in your case are many or if they are complex, such as custody, the attorney's fees and other costs of going to trial can be tremendous. By settling your case without going to trial, you may be able to save thousands of dollars in legal fees. Ask your attorney for a litigation estimate setting forth the potential costs of trial, so that you have an idea of these costs when deciding whether to settle an issue or to take it to trial before the judge.

6.5 Are there other benefits to mediating or negotiating a settlement?

Yes. A divorce resolved by a mediated or negotiated agreement can have these additional benefits:

Recognizing Common Goals. Mediation and negotiation allow for brainstorming between the parties and attorneys. Looking at all possible solutions, even impractical ones, invites creative solutions to common goals. For example, suppose you and your spouse both agree you need to pay your spouse some amount of equity for the family home you will keep, but you have no cash to make the payment. Together, you may come up with a number of options for accomplishing your goal and select the best one. Contrast this with a judge who simply orders you to pay the money without considering all of the possible options.

Addressing the Unique Circumstances of Your Situation. Rather than using a one-size-fits-all approach as a judge might, a settlement reached by agreement allows you and your spouse to consider the unique circumstances of your situation in formulating a good outcome. For example, suppose you disagree about parenting times for the Thanksgiving holiday. The judge might order you to alternate the holiday each year, although you both would have preferred to have your child share the day.

Creating a Safe Place for Communication. Mediation and negotiation give each party an opportunity to be heard. Perhaps you and your spouse have not yet had an opportunity to directly share your concerns about settlement with one another. For example, you may be worried about how the temporary parenting time arrangement is impacting your children, but have not yet discussed it with your spouse. A mediation session or settlement conference can be a safe place for the two of you to communicate concerns about your children or your finances.

Fulfilling Your Children's Needs. You may see that your children would be better served by you and your spouse deciding their future rather than having it decided by a judge who does not know, love, and understand your children like the two of you do.

Eliminating the Risk and Uncertainty of Trial. If a judge decides the outcome of your divorce, you give up control over the terms of the settlement. The decisions are left in the hands of the judge. If you and your spouse reach agreement, however, you have the power to eliminate the risk of an uncertain outcome.

Reducing the Risk of Harm to Your Children. If your case goes to trial, it is likely you and your spouse will give testimony that will be upsetting to each other. As the conflict increases, the relationship between you and your spouse inevitably deteriorates. This can be harmful to your children. Contrast this with mediation or settlement negotiations, in which you open your communication and seek to reach agreement. It is not unusual for the relationship between the parents to improve as the professionals create a safe environment for rebuilding communication and reaching agreements in the best interest of a child.

Having the Support of Professionals. Using trained professionals, such as mediators and attorneys, to support you can help you to reach a settlement you may think is impossible. These professionals have skills to help you focus on what is most important to you, and shift your attention away from irrelevant facts. They understand the law and know the possible outcomes if your case goes to trial.

Lowering Stress. The process of preparing for and going to court can be stressful. Your energy is also going toward caring for your children, looking at your finances, and coping with the emotions of divorce. You might decide you would be better served by settling your case rather than proceeding to trial.

Achieving Closure. When you are going through a divorce, the process can feel as though it is taking an eternity. By reaching agreement, you and your spouse are better able to put the divorce behind you and move forward with your lives.

6.6   Is mediation mandatory?
It depends on the county of your residence. Mediation is not mandatory prior to filing for divorce, but mediation can be mandatory in some counties prior to being allowed to proceed

to trial. In other counties, mediation is only mandatory prior to trial if you have minor children. Some counties have no mediation requirements. Mandatory mediation is more likely in heavily populated counties with a significant family law caseload. Even in counties with mandatory mediation, exceptions can be made for domestic violence situations. Ask your attorney what your county's mediation requirements are.

6.7 My spouse was mentally or physically abusive to me. Should I participate in mediation anyway?

If you have been a victim of domestic violence by your spouse, it is important that you discuss the appropriateness of mediation with your attorney. Mediation may not be a safe way for you to reach an agreement. This is particularly true if you have a protection order against your spouse or have been a victim of stalking and other harassing conduct.

Prior to allowing mediation to proceed, any mediator should ask whether you have been a victim of domestic violence. This is critical for the mediator in both assessing your safety and ensuring the balance of power in the mediation process is maintained. If you decide to proceed with mediation, at the very least you and your spouse should be in different rooms with no contact, or mediate during separate, individual sessions. Your attorney should also be present with you during the mediation process.

6.8 What training and credentials do mediators have?

The background of mediators varies. Most mediators are attorneys or retired judges, while others have counseling backgrounds. Most mediators have attended significant mediation training which is offered both in and out of state.

Many counties maintain a list of approved mediators. You can contact the county clerk and ask if such a list exists. You should select a mediator with extensive experience in family law matters. Your attorney will know who the most qualified mediators in your area are.

6.9   What types of issues can be mediated or negotiated?

All of the issues in your case can be mediated or negotiated. However, in advance of any mediation or negotiation session, you should discuss with your attorney which issues you want to be mediated or negotiated. It is important to meet with your attorney before the mediation to ensure you have similar goals and a similar agenda for the mediation.

You may decide certain issues are nonnegotiable. Discuss this with your attorney in advance of any mediation or negotiation sessions so he or she can support you in focusing the discussions on the issues you are open to mediating. Before mediation, it is wise to set limits on how far you are willing to compromise. That way, in the heat of the mediation moment when the "last, best settlement offer" is being presented, you will not accept a settlement you would be very unhappy with later, after the stress of the situation has worn off and you can think without pressure.

6.10   What is the role of my attorney in the mediation process?

The role of your attorney in the mediation process will vary depending upon your situation. Your attorney can assist you in identifying which issues will be discussed in mediation and which are better left to negotiation between the attorneys or to the judge. While some attorneys will allow their clients to go to mediation alone, this author thinks that this is a serious error. Why make potentially life-altering decisions without the benefits of having your attorney present? Further, why should you be left to negotiate when this is precisely what your attorney is trained to do? Insist on your attorney being present for the entirety of mediation. If your attorney is disinterested or unwilling to participate, find new counsel.

6.11   How do I prepare for mediation?

Prior to attending a mediation session with your spouse, discuss with your attorney the issues you intend to mediate. In particular, be sure to discuss the impact of custody and parenting time arrangements.

Be forward looking. Give thought to your desired outcome. Decide in advance which issues are most important to you, and which issues you are willing to compromise on.

6.12 Do children attend the mediation sessions?

In virtually all cases your child will not participate in the mediation. Mediation is for the spouses and their respective attorneys. On occasion, the attorneys may agree to allow third parties such as parents, siblings, or friends to participate.

6.13 Who pays for mediation?

The cost of mediation must be paid for by you and/or your spouse. Often mediation is a shared expense. Expect your mediator to address the matter of fees before or at your first session. Your attorney should have this arranged in advance, although the payment of these fees is sometimes an issue negotiated in the mediation.

6.14 What if mediation fails?

If mediation is unsuccessful, you may still be able to settle your case through negotiations between the attorneys. If there appears to be some hope for resolution, an additional mediation session can be scheduled or a different mediator utilized. Also, you and your spouse can agree to preserve the settlements reached and take only the remaining disputed issues to the judge for trial.

6.15 What is a *settlement conference*?

A *settlement conference* is a meeting held with you, your spouse, and your attorneys with the intention of negotiating the terms of your divorce. It can be a powerful tool for the resolution of your case. It In some cases, a professional with important information needed to support the settlement process, such as an accountant, also may participate. Settlement conferences are most effective when both parties and their attorneys see the potential for a negotiated resolution and have the necessary information to accomplish this goal.

In some counties, a judicial officer may conduct formal settlement conferences. In such a situation, the judicial officer attempts to help the parties settle their case informally. There is no requirement for the parties to agree. Because of budget constraints, this process has been phased out of many counties.

6.16 Why should I consider a settlement conference when the attorneys can negotiate through letters and phone calls?

A settlement conference can eliminate delays that often occur when negotiation takes place through correspondence and calls between attorneys. In a settlement conference you can receive a response on a proposal in a matter of minutes, rather than waiting days or weeks. A settlement conference also enables you and your spouse to use your own words to explain the reasoning behind your requests. You are also able to provide information immediately to expedite the process.

6.17 How do I prepare for my settlement conference?

Being well prepared for the settlement conference can help you make the most of this opportunity to resolve your case without the need for trial. Actions you should take include:

- Provide in advance of the conference all necessary information. If your attorney has asked you for a current pay stub, tax return, debt amounts, asset values, or other documentation, make sure it is provided prior to the meeting.

- Discuss your topics of concern with your attorney in advance. Your attorney can assist you in understanding your rights under the law so you can have realistic expectations for the outcome of negotiations.

- Bring a positive attitude, a listening ear, and an open mind. Come with the attitude that your case will settle. Be willing to listen to the opposing party. Resist the urge to interrupt.

Few cases settle without each side demonstrating flexibility and a willingness to compromise. Most cases settle when parties are able to bring these positive qualities to the process.

6.18 What will happen at my settlement conference?

Typically the conference will be held at the office of one of the attorneys, with both parties and attorneys present. If there are a number of issues to be discussed, an agenda may be used to keep the focus on relevant topics. From time to time throughout the conference, you and your attorney may meet alone to consult as needed. If additional information is needed to reach an agreement, some issues may be set aside for later discussion.

The length of the conference depends upon the number of issues to be resolved, the complexity of the issues, and the willingness of the parties and attorneys to communicate effectively. An effort is made to confirm which issues are resolved and which issues remain disputed. Then, one by one, the issues are addressed.

6.19 What is the role of my attorney in the settlement conference?

Your attorney is your advocate during the settlement conference. You can count on him or her to support you throughout the process and ensure important issues are addressed. Your attorney should also counsel you privately outside the presence of your spouse and his or her attorney.

6.20 Why is my attorney appearing so friendly with my spouse and her attorney?

Successful negotiations rely upon building trust between the parties working toward agreement. Your attorney may be respectful or pleasant toward your spouse or your spouse's attorney to promote a good outcome for you. Where attorneys are rude, threatening, or condescending, settlements are far less likely to occur.

6.21 What happens if my spouse and I settled some but not all of the issues in our divorce?

You and your spouse can agree to maintain the agreements you have reached and let the judge decide those matters that you are unable to resolve.

6.22   If my spouse and I reach an agreement, how long will it take before it can be finalized?

If a settlement is reached through negotiation or mediation, one of the attorneys will put the agreement in writing for approval by you and your spouse. These documents can usually be prepared in about a week depending on the attorney's schedule. Assuming you have met the required ninety-day waiting period, your divorce can be finalized as soon as all necessary documents have been signed by both sides. No hearings are required where the divorce documents are based on agreement of the parties.

7

Emergency:
When You Fear Your Spouse

Suddenly you are in a panic. Maybe your spouse was serious when threatening to take your child and leave the state. What if you are kicked out of your own home? Suppose all of the bank accounts are emptied. Your fear heightens as your mind spins with every horror story you have heard about divorce.

Facing an emergency situation in divorce can feel as though your entire life is at stake. You may not be able to concentrate on anything else. At the same time, you may be paralyzed with anxiety and have no idea how to begin to protect yourself. No doubt you have countless worries about what your future holds.

Remember, you have overcome many challenges in your life before this moment. There are people willing to help you. Step by step, you will make it through again this time. When facing an emergency, do your best to focus on what to do in the immediate moment. Set aside your worries about the future for another day. Let others support you, and start taking action right away.

7.1 My spouse has deserted me, and I need to get divorced as quickly as possible. What is my first step?

Your first step is to seek legal advice at your earliest opportunity. The earlier you get legal counsel to advise you about your rights, the better. The initial consultation with an attorney will answer most of your questions and start you on an action plan for getting your divorce underway.

7.2   I'm afraid my abusive spouse will try to hurt me and/ or our children if I say I want a divorce. What can I do legally to protect myself and my children?

Develop a plan with your safety and that of your children as your highest priority. In addition to meeting with an attorney at your first opportunity, develop a safety plan in the event you and your children need to escape your home. A great way to do this is to let in support from an agency that helps victims of domestic violence. The YWCA, the courts, and other agencies have wonderful counselors ready to assist you. Call them.

Your risk of harm from an abusive spouse increases when you leave. For this reason, all actions must be taken with safety as the first concern. Find an attorney who understands domestic violence. Often, your local domestic violence agency can help with a referral. Talk to your attorney about the concerns for your safety and that of your children. Ask your attorney about a *protection order*. This is a court order that may offer a number of protections including granting you temporary custody of your children, ordering your spouse to leave the family residence, and ordering your spouse to have no contact with you. A spouse who violates these orders faces immediate arrest and subsequent prosecution. Be assured that the courts take domestic violence very seriously.

7.3   I am afraid to meet with an attorney because I am terrified my spouse will find out and get violent. What should I do?

Schedule an initial consultation with an attorney who is experienced in working with domestic violence victims. When you schedule the appointment, let the firm know your situation and instruct the law office not to place any calls to you that you think your spouse might discover. If possible, pay for your consultation in cash.

Consultations with your attorney are confidential. Your attorney has an ethical duty to not disclose your meeting with anyone outside the law firm. Let your attorney know your concerns so extra precautions can be taken by the law office in handling your file.

7.4 I want to give my attorney all the information needed so my children and I are safe from my spouse. What does this include?

Provide your attorney with complete information about the history, background, nature, and evidence of your abuse including:

- Types of abuse (for example, physical, sexual, verbal, financial, mental, emotional)
- Dates, time frames, or occasions
- The locations
- Whether you were ever medically treated
- Any police reports made
- E-mails, letters, notes, or journal entries
- Photographs taken
- Witnesses to the abuse or evidence of the abuse
- Statements made by your spouse admitting the abuse
- Alcohol or drug abuse
- The presence of guns or other weapons

The better the information you provide to your attorney, the easier it will be for him or her to make a strong case for the protection of you and your children.

7.5 I'm not ready to hire an attorney for a divorce, but I am afraid my spouse is going to get violent with my children and me in the meantime. What can I do?

You can seek a protection order from the court without an attorney. It is possible for the judge to order your spouse out of your home, grant you interim custody of your children, and order your spouse to stay away from you.

7.6 What is the difference between a *domestic violence protection order,* an *anti-harassment protection order,* and a *restraining order*?

Protection orders and restraining orders are court orders directing a person to not engage in certain behavior. Each is intended to protect others. Although any of the orders can initially be obtained without notice to the other person, there is always a right to a hearing to determine whether a protection order or restraining order should remain in place.

Domestic Violence Protection Order. Talk to your attorney about obtaining a domestic violence protection order if you are concerned about your safety, your children's safety, or if there has been a history of domestic abuse. If your spouse has attempted or threatened to cause you bodily injury, or has actually caused you bodily injury, you will likely qualify for a domestic violence protection order. The violation of a domestic abuse protection order is a criminal offense, which can result in immediate arrest.

Anti-Harassment Protection Order. If your spouse has engaged in conduct that seriously harasses or intimidates you, speak with your attorney about the possibility of obtaining an anti-harassment protection order. Following, stalking, or repeatedly contacting you are examples of harassment that may qualify for protection. The violation of an anti-harassment protection order is also a criminal offense, which can result in an immediate arrest.

Restraining Order. If you are concerned your spouse will annoy, threaten, harass, or intimidate you after your divorce complaint is filed, ask your attorney about a restraining order. A restraining order is a court order that prohibits a person from engaging in behavior that has been restrained by the court. If your spouse violates the restraining order, he or she may be brought before the court for contempt.

7.7 My spouse has never been violent, but I know she is going to be really angry and upset when the divorce papers are served. Do I need a protection order?

The facts of your case may not warrant a protection order. However, if you are still concerned about your spouse's behavior, ask your attorney about a *temporary restraining order (TRO)* to be delivered to your spouse at the same time as the divorce complaint. This court order directs your spouse not to annoy, threaten, intimidate, or harass you while the divorce is in progress. A temporary restraining order can also order your spouse not to sell or transfer assets until your divorce is completed.

7.8 My spouse has been harassing me since I filed for divorce. What can I do?

It may be possible to seek a harassment protection order from the court. In order to qualify for a harassment protection order, you must be able to prove that your spouse has engaged in a knowing and willful course of conduct that seriously harasses, threatens, or intimidates you. Talk with your attorney about whether you should seek the court's protection from your spouse.

7.9 I'm afraid my spouse is going to take all of the money out of the bank accounts and leave me with nothing. What can I do?

Talk to your attorney immediately. If you are worried about your spouse emptying financial accounts or selling marital assets, it is critical that you take action at once. Your attorney can advise you on your right to take possession of certain assets in order to protect them from being hidden or spent by your spouse.

Talk to your attorney about the benefits of obtaining a temporary restraining order as to property prior to giving your spouse notice that you are filing for divorce.

This order forbids your spouse from selling, transferring, hiding, or otherwise disposing of marital property until the divorce is complete. A temporary restraining order is intended to prevent assets from "disappearing" before a final division of the property from your marriage is complete.

7.10 My spouse says I am crazy, a liar, and that no judge will ever believe me if I tell the truth about the abusive behavior. What can I do if I don't have any proof?

Most domestic violence is not witnessed by third parties. Often there is little physical evidence. Even without physical evidence, a judge can enter orders to protect you and your children if you give truthful testimony about your abuse which the judge finds believable. Your own testimony of your abuse is evidence.

It is very common for persons who abuse others to claim the victim is a liar and to make statements intended to discourage disclosure of the abuse. This is yet another form of controlling behavior. Your attorney's skills and experience will support you to give effective testimony in the courtroom to establish your case. Let your attorney know your concerns so a strong case can be presented to the judge based upon your persuasive statements of the truth of your experience.

7.11 My spouse told me that if I ever file for divorce, I'll never see my child again. Should I be worried about my child being abducted?

Your fear that your spouse will abduct your child is a common one. However, abductions across state lines, or even hiding out within the state, are rare because of the consequences that will surely occur. Depending on the severity and length of the abduction, consequences can range from contempt of court, to loss of parenting time with the child, to significant imprisonment. If you suspect your spouse may be planning to abduct your child, or if there are risk factors present, talk with your attorney. He or she can work with the courts to obtain restraints and other protections that help lower the risk of abduction.

It can be helpful to look at some of the factors that appear to increase the risk that your child will be removed from the state by the other parent.

One risk factor for abduction is marriages that are mixed race, religions, cultures, or ethnicities. A prior criminal record, or pending serious criminal charges that carry the threat of significant imprisonment, can increase the risk. Another factor increasing this risk is a party's limited social or economic ties to the community. Threats to flee or a sudden change in financial affairs or employment are risk factors as well.

The greatest concern exists where your spouse has significant contacts in a foreign country. It can be very difficult and very costly to work with a foreign country to have your child returned to you. This is particularly true with countries such as Japan and some Middle Eastern countries. In these countries, obtaining the return of your child can be nearly impossible. In cases with potential foreign country issues, you should work closely with your attorney to secure passports and monitor the conduct of your spouse. Considerable thought should be given to placing provisions in your parenting plan that decrease the risk of abduction. Any actions by your spouse that indicate that he or she may be leaving to this foreign country should be immediately brought to the attention of your attorney.

7.12 What legal steps can be taken to prevent my spouse from removing our child from the state?

If you are concerned about your child being removed from the state, ask your attorney whether any of these options might be available in your case:

- A court order giving you immediate custody until a temporary custody hearing can be held
- A court order directing your spouse to turn over passports for the child and your spouse to the court
- The posting of a bond prior to your spouse exercising parenting time
- Supervised visitation

Both state and federal laws are designed to provide protection from the removal of children from one state to another when a custody matter is brought and to protect children from kidnapping. *The Uniform Child Custody Jurisdiction Enforcement Act (UCCJEA)* was passed to encourage the custody of children to be decided in the state where they have been living most recently and where they have the most ties. *The Parental Kidnapping Prevention Act (PKPA)* makes it a federal crime for a parent to kidnap a child in violation of a valid custody order.

7.13 How quickly can I get a divorce in Washington?

As mentioned earlier, after you file your divorce, your spouse must be served with the summons and petition for dissolution. Other documents may be served as appropriate. A ninety-day waiting period is required for every Washington divorce. This period begins once the divorce is filed with the court *and* your spouse has been served. Assuming that you and your spouse have reached agreement on all issues, your divorce can be finalized once the ninety-day waiting period is complete.

7.14 I really need a divorce quickly. Will the divorce I get in another country be valid in Washington?

If both you and your spouse regard Washington as your true home and you both intend to remain in the state, a divorce from another country may not be valid. Even if your spouse joins you in filing in a foreign country, the decree may possibly be vacated at a later date (called a "set aside"). Trying to get around the laws of Washington often causes more problems than are solved by a "quickie divorce." Talk to an attorney before considering such actions.

7.15 If either my spouse or I file for divorce, will I be ordered out of my home? Who decides who gets to live in the house while we go through the divorce?

If you and your spouse, with the assistance of your attorneys, cannot reach an agreement regarding which of you will leave the residence during the divorce, the judge will decide whether one of you should be granted exclusive possession of the home until the case is concluded. However, in some cases judges have been known to refuse to order either party out of the house until the divorce is concluded.

Abusive behavior is one basis for seeking temporary possession of the home. If there are minor children, the custodial parent will ordinarily be awarded temporary possession of the residence. Other factors the judge may consider include:

- Whether one of you owned the home prior to the marriage
- After provisions are made for payment of temporary support, who can afford to remain in the home or obtain other housing
- Who is most likely to be awarded the home in the divorce
- Options available to each of you for other temporary housing, including other homes or family members who live in the area
- Special needs that would make a move unduly burdensome, such as a health condition
- Self-employment from home, which could not be readily moved, such as a child-care business

If staying in the home is important to you, talk to your attorney about your reasons so a strong case can be made for you at the temporary hearing. It is highly advisable to not move out of your home unless advised to do so by your attorney. Moving out of the home can cause serious consequences for your parenting plan and financial orders.

8

Child Custody

Ever since you and your spouse began talking about divorce, chances are your children have been your greatest concern. You or your spouse might have postponed the decision to seek a divorce because of concerns over the impact on your children. Now that the time has come, you might still have doubts about whether your children will be all right after the divorce.

Remember, you have been making wise and loving decisions for your children since they were born. You have done your best to ensure they had everything they needed. You loved them and protected them. This will not change because you are going through a divorce. You were a good parent before the divorce and you will still be a good parent after it. But it can understandably be difficult to not worry about how the sharing of parenting time with your spouse will affect your children.

You may also have fears about being cut out of your child's life. Try to remember that regardless of who has custody, it is likely the court order will not only give you time with your children but also a generous opportunity to be involved in their day-to-day lives. With the help of your attorney, you can make sound decisions regarding the custody arrangement that is in the best interests of your children.

8.1   What types of custody are awarded in Washington?

Under Washington law, physical custody is determined by which parent has the majority of the residential time with the child in a given year. If you have more than 50 percent of the residential time, you will be the custodial parent. Joint custody is also recognized. Joint custody occurs when each parent has exactly 50 percent of the residential time with the child.

Joint legal custody is not frequently awarded by the courts. It is often discouraged unless certain factors are present, such as:

- Effective an open communication between the parents concerning the child

- A strong desire on the part of both parents to continue to co-parent together

- A history of active involvement of bother parents in the child's life

- Similar parenting values held by both parents

- A willingness on the part of both parents to place the child's needs before their own

- Both parents' willingness to be flexible and compromising about making decisions concerning the child

Specific parenting time will always be awarded to each parent, regardless of who has physical custody, unless circumstances exist that call for restrictions of a parent's residential time. Factors causing restriction can be abuse, domestic violence, drug and/or alcohol issues, or abandonment. Otherwise, provisions for sharing of the school schedule, school breaks, summer, holidays, and vacations are typically made in detail.

8.2   On what basis will the judge award custody?

The judge considers many factors in determining child custody. Most important is "the best interests of the child." To determine best interests, the judge may look at the following factors:

Home Environments. This refers to the respective environments offered by you and your spouse. The court may consider factors such as the safety, stability, and nurturing found in each home.

Emotional Ties. The emotional relationship between the child and each parent may include the nature of the bond between the parent and child and the feelings shared between the child and each parent.

Age, Sex, and Health of the Child and Parents. Washington no longer ascribes to the "tender years" doctrine, which formerly gave a preference for custody of very young children to the mother. If one of the parents has an illness that may impair the ability to parent, it may be considered by the court. Similarly, the judge may look at special health needs of a child.

Effect on the Child of Continuing or Disrupting an Existing Relationship. This factor might be applied in your case if you stayed at home for a period of years to care for your child, and awarding custody to the other parent would disrupt your relationship with your child.

Attitude and Stability of Each Parent's Character. The court may consider your ability and willingness to be cooperative with the other parent in deciding who should be awarded custody. The court may also consider each parent's history, which reflects the stability of his or her character.

Moral Fitness of Each Parent, Including Sexual Conduct. The extent to which a judge assesses the morals of a parent can vary greatly from judge to judge. Your own sexual conduct is ordinarily not considered unless it has harmed your child or your child was exposed to such sexual conduct.

Capacity to Provide Physical Care and Satisfy Educational Needs. Here, the court may examine whether you or the other parent is better able to provide for your child's daily needs such as nutrition, health care, hygiene, social activities, and education. The court may also look to see whether you or your spouse has been attending to these needs in the past.

Preferences of the Child. The child's preference regarding custody may be considered if the child is of sufficient age of comprehension, regardless of chronological age, and the child's preference is based on sound reasoning. Washington, unlike some other states, does not allow a child to choose the parent he or she wishes to live with. Rather, the court may consider the well-reasoned preferences of a child, at any age. Typically, the older the child is, the greater the weight given to the preference. However, the child's reasoning is also important. Keep in mind that the courts do not like to involve children in the litigation process, so the wishes of the child may not be a factor a particular judge is willing to consider.

Health, Welfare, and Social Behavior of the Child. Every child is unique. Your child's needs must be considered when it comes to deciding custody and parenting time. The custody of a child with special needs, for example, may be awarded to the parent who is better able to meet those needs. The judge may also consider whether you or your spouse has fulfilled the role of primary care provider for meeting the child's day-to-day needs.

Domestic Violence. Domestic violence is an important factor in determining custody, parenting time, and protection from abuse during the transfer of your child to the other parent. If domestic violence is a concern in your case, be sure to discuss it in detail with your attorney during the initial consultation so every measure can be taken to protect the safety of you and your children.

8.3 What's the difference between *visitation* and *residential time*?

Historically, time spent with the noncustodial parent was referred to as *visitation.* Today, the term *residential time* is more often used to refer to the time a child spends with either parent.

This change in language reflects the intention that children spend time with both parents and have two homes, as opposed to living with one parent and visiting the other.

8.4 How can I make sure I will get to keep the children during the divorce proceedings?

You cannot absolutely ensure your children will stay with you during the divorce process. However, a temporary order is the best way to provide clarity about the living arrangements and respective parenting time with your children during the divorce. Informal agreements between parties cannot always be trusted and any informal agreement made with your spouse lacks the ability to be enforced by the court. Thus, even if you and your spouse have agreed to temporary arrangements, talk with your attorney about whether this agreement should be formalized in a court order.

Obtaining a temporary order can be an important protection not only for the custody of your children, but also for other issues such as support, temporary exclusive possession of the marital home, temporary protection from your spouse, or attorney fees. Until a temporary order is entered, it is best for you continue to reside with your children. If you are considering leaving your home, talk with your attorney before making any significant changes. If you must leave your home, take your children with you (if you have been the primary caretaker and such actions will be best for your children) and talk with your attorney at the earliest opportunity.

8.5   How much weight does the child's preference carry?

The preference of your child is only one of many factors a judge may consider in determining custody. The age of your child and his or her ability to express the underlying reason for their preference will determine the amount of weight a judge will give to this preference. Although there is no age at which your child's preference influences parenting plan decisions, most judges give more weight to the wishes of an older child. Generally, the preference of a high-school-age child carries more weight than that of a younger child. If a child is younger than junior high school age, a judge is unlikely to give his or her preference much consideration unless it is expressed through a qualified counselor.

The reasoning underlying your child's preference is also a factor to consider. Consider the fifteen-year-old girl who wants to live with her mother because "Mom lets me stay out past curfew, I get a bigger allowance, and I don't have to do chores." Greater weight might be given to the preference of a fifteen-year-old who wants to live with her mother because "she helps me with my homework, supports my extracurricular activities, and has a quiet home where I can study without interruption." If you feel that your child's preference may be a factor in the determination of custody, discuss it with your attorney so this consideration is a part of assessing the action to be taken in your case.

8.6 How old do the children have to be before they can speak to the judge about with whom they want to live?

First, it is unlikely the judge will want to speak with your child. The courts are fairly uniform in wanting to keep children out of litigation. On the rare occasion the judge feels speaking with a child may be helpful or required, the judge is more likely to speak with a child who is at least of junior high age. More typically, the judge will use a guardian *ad litem* or a counselor for this purpose.

8.7 How can I prove that I was the primary care provider?

One tool to assist you and your attorney in establishing your case as a primary care provider is a chart indicating the care you and your spouse have each provided for your child. The clearer you are about the history of parenting, the better job your attorney can do in presenting your case to the judge. Look at the activities in the chart below to help review the role of you and your spouse as care providers for your child.

Parental Roles Chart

Activity	Mother	Father
Attended prenatal medical visits		
Attended prenatal class		
Took time off work after child was born		
Got up with child at feedings		
Got up with child when sick at night		
Bathed child		
Put child to sleep		
Potty-trained child		
Prepared and fed meals to child		
Helped child learn numbers, letters, colors, etc.		
Helped child learn to read		
Helped child with practice for music, dance lessons, sports		

Parental Roles Chart (Continued)

Activity	Mother	Father
Took time off work with sick child		
Took child to doctor visits		
Went to pharmacy for child's medication		
Administered child's medication		
Took child to therapy		
Took child to optometrist		
Took child to dentist		
Took child to get haircuts		
Bought clothing for child		
Bought school supplies for child		
Transported child to school		
Picked up child after school		
Drove carpool for child's school		
Went to child's school activities		
Helped child with homework and projects		
Attended parent-teacher conferences		
Chaperoned child's school trips and activities		
Transported child to day care		
Communicated with day care providers		
Transported child from day care		
Attended day care activities		
Signed child up for sports, dance, music		
Bought equipment for sports, dance, music		
Transported child to sports, dance, music		
Attended sports, dance, music practices		
Attended sports, dance, music recitals		
Coached child's sports		
Transported child from sports, dance, music		

Parental Roles Chart (Continued)

Activity	Mother	Father
Knows child's friends and friends' families		
Took child to religious education		
Participated in child's religious education		
Obtained information and training about special needs of child		
Comforted child during times of emotional upset		

8.8 Do I have to let my spouse see the children before we are actually divorced?

Unless your children are at risk for being harmed by your spouse, your children should maintain reasonable contact with the other parent. It is important for children to experience the presence of both parents in their lives, regardless of the parents' separation. Even if there is no temporary order for parenting time, cooperate with your spouse in making reasonable arrangements for time with your children. You should, however, discuss this with your attorney to ensure the decisions you make do not harm your case.

When safety is not an issue, if you deny contact with the other parent prior to trial, your judge is likely to question whether you have the best interests of your child at heart. This is especially true if you are found in contempt of court for denying contact. Talk to your attorney about what parenting schedule would be best for your children on a temporary basis. Obtain a temporary parenting plan from the court so you do not sit in limbo and are certain of what to do during your separation.

8.9 I am seeing a counselor or psychologist. Will that hurt my chances of getting custody?

If you are seeing a counselor, first acknowledge yourself for getting the professional support you need. Your well-being is important to your ability to be the best parent you can be. Discuss with your attorney the implications of your being treated by a therapist. It is probable the condition for which you are being treated in no way affects your child or your ability to be a loving and supportive parent. The courts often look favorably upon parents who turn to counseling to deal with the stresses of the separation process so they can make good decisions going forward.

Your mental health records may be subpoenaed by the other parent's attorney. For this reason it is important to discuss with your attorney an action plan for responding to a request to obtain records in your therapist's file. Ask your attorney to contact your therapist to alert him or her regarding how to respond to a request for your mental health records.

8.10 I am taking prescription medication to treat my depression. Will this hurt my chances of getting custody?

Not usually. Feelings of depression, anxiety, and trouble sleeping are common during a divorce. If you have any mental health concerns, seek help from a professional. Following through with the recommendations made by your health care provider will be looked favorably upon by the court, including the use of prescription medication. Discuss the best way to proceed with counseling with your attorney.

If your depression is so severe that you have trouble functioning during the day, this could impact your parenting time. Other mental health issues can also impact parenting time. However, it is generally far better to address these issues so the court is assured the matter is under control, rather than to try to hide it. It is important to discuss with your attorney the best way to resolve these issues so your parenting time is not impacted.

8.11 Will my children be present if we go to court?

Generally, the answer is no. Judges make every effort to protect minor children from the conflict of the parents. For this reason, most judges will not allow minor children to be present in the courtroom to hear the testimony of other witnesses or of the parents. The only exception would be if a judge decided to speak with a minor child. Adult children, however, are generally allowed to be present if they so desire as Washington law promotes open courtrooms.

8.12 Should I hire a private detective to prove my spouse is having an affair?

It is rarely needed to hire a private detective for this purpose. Washington is a "no-fault" state and the existence of an affair is generally not relevant to the judge. The only exceptions may be where assets are being transferred to this other individual, or where this other individual has a criminal history or moral character issue that may endanger your child.

8.13 Will the fact that I had an affair during the marriage hurt my chances of getting custody?

Whether an affair will have any impact on your custody case depends upon many factors, including:

- Whether the children were exposed to sexual activities
- Whether the affair had any emotional impact on the children
- Whether the other individual has issues with domestic violence, criminal history, drug use, or other moral character concerns

In determining custody, a court may consider the parent's moral fitness, which includes his or her sexual activity. This is not strictly limited to affairs, but may also include pornography use. However, these considerations will only be taken into account if the children were exposed to sexual activity or were adversely affected by the exposure to an affair or pornography. If you had an affair during your marriage or have had issues with pornography, discuss these issues with your attorney at the outset so you can assess their impact, if any, on custody. In most circumstances, they will be irrelevant.

8.14 During the months it takes to get a divorce is it okay to date or will it hurt my chances at custody?

If custody is disputed, talk with your attorney about your plans to begin dating. Your dating may be irrelevant if the children are unaware of it. However, most judges will frown upon exposing your children to a new relationship when they are still adjusting to the separation of their parents. If your spouse is contesting custody, it may be best to focus your energy on your children, the litigation, and taking care of yourself.

If you do date and become sexually involved with your new partner, it is imperative your children not be exposed to any sexual activity. If they are, it could harm your case for custody. You must also ensure your new partner is of high moral character. Issues with drugs, alcohol, domestic violence, or a criminal history could harm your custody case.

8.15 Can having a live-in partner hurt my chances of getting custody?

If you are contemplating having your partner live with you, first discuss this decision with your attorney. If you are already living with your partner, let your attorney know immediately so the potential impact on any custody ruling can be assessed. Your living with someone who is not your spouse may have significant impact on your custody case, particularly if this new partner is not well liked by your children.

However, judges' opinions of the significance of this factor can vary greatly. Talk promptly and frankly with your attorney. It will be important for you to look together at many aspects, including the following:

- How the judge assigned to your case views this situation
- Whether your living arrangement is likely to prompt a custody dispute that would not otherwise arise
- How long you have been separated from the other parent
- How long you have been in a relationship with your new partner
- The history and nature of the children's relationship with your partner
- Whether your partner has moral character concerns such as drug or alcohol use, domestic violence history, or a criminal history
- Your future plans with your partner (such as marriage)

Living with a partner may put your custody case at risk. At the very least, it may cause your spouse to extend the litigation and cause you thousands of dollars in avoidable attorney fees. Consider such a decision thoughtfully, taking into account the advice of your attorney. If living with a new partner can wait until after your case is complete, you will generally be better served.

8.16 I'm gay and came out to my spouse when I filed for divorce. What impact will my sexual orientation have on my case for custody or parenting time?

There are no laws in Washington that impact or limit your rights as a parent based upon your sexual orientation. Sexual activity by a parent is generally an insignificant factor in determining custody. However, exposing your child to sexual activity or engaging in sexual activity that harms your child are relevant factors in a custody dispute. Be sure to choose an attorney you are confident will fully support you in your goals as a parent.

8.17 How is *abandonment* defined legally and how might it affect the outcome of our custody dispute?

Abandonment is rarely an issue in custody litigation unless one parent has been absent from the child's life for an extended period. Being absent for a few weeks is unlikely to be a significant issue in obtaining residential time, but it could certainly impact custody. Under Washington law, the courts look to see if there is a lack of significant contact between a parent and a child. This is determined by the facts and circumstances of each case. The intentional absence of a parent's presence, care, protection, and support are all considered.

8.18 Can I have witnesses file declarations or speak on my behalf to try to get custody of my children?

Absolutely. Witnesses are critical in every custody case. At a temporary hearing, a witness is more likely to provide testimony by declaration or affidavit, which is a written, sworn statement. However, at a trial for the final determination of custody, you and the other parent will each have an opportunity to present witnesses who will give live testimony on your behalf.

Among those you might consider as potential witnesses in your custody case are:

- Family members, particularly if they are family members of your spouse and they are willing to help you. This is very powerful evidence. Evidence from your own mother or father is far less persuasive and is usually avoided unless you have no other corroborating witnesses or if they have very specific knowledge (have provided child care, for example).
- Family friends
- Child-care providers
- Neighbors
- Teachers
- Health care providers
- Clergy members

In determining which witnesses would best support your case, your attorney may consider the following:

- What is the witness's opportunity to observe you or the other parent, especially with your child?
- How frequently? How recently?
- How long has the witness known you or the other parent?
- What is the relationship of the witness to the child and the parents?
- How valuable is the knowledge that this witness has?
- Does this witness have knowledge different from that of other witnesses?
- Is the witness available and willing to testify?
- Is the witness clear in conveying information?
- Is the witness credible, that is, will the judge believe this witness?
- Does the witness have any biases or prejudices that could impact the testimony?

You and your attorney can work together to determine which witnesses will best support your case. Support your attorney by providing a list of potential witnesses together with your opinion regarding the answers to the above questions.

Give your attorney the phone numbers, addresses, and workplaces of each of your potential witnesses.

Your attorney should draft the declarations of your witnesses. Handwritten declarations prepared by the witnesses or declarations prepared by you will not be as effective. If your attorney is reluctant to prepare the declarations, consider immediately changing attorneys. Quality declarations are probably the most important factor in obtaining temporary custody. They should be given the utmost attention.

8.19   Will my attorney want to speak with my children?

In most cases your attorney will not ask to speak with your children. If your attorney develops excessive contact with your child, the court may have concerns that the child was potentially influenced by the attorney. Additionally, judges frown on children being exposed to litigation, and your attorney is part of the litigation process. For this reason it is better to not bring your child to your attorney's office. Where input from the child is appropriate, it is almost always better to enlist the services of a qualified counselor.

8.20   Who serves as a guardian *ad litem*? Why is one appointed?

The guardian *ad litem* (sometimes referred to as the "GAL"), is typically an attorney or counselor, directed by the judge to conduct an investigation into the issue of custody or residential time for a parent. The guardian *ad litem* is typically selected from a list of individuals who have been approved by the state's Superior Court. These individuals have generally undertaken special training in order to be qualified to serve as guardians *ad litem*. Each county has different procedures for the selection of a guardian *ad litem* and you will certainly want to discuss with your attorney which guardian *ad litem* would be most appropriate for the issues of your case.

A guardian *ad litem* may be appointed to specifically investigate mental health issues, *Child Protective Services (CPS)* involvement, or concerns over drug or alcohol use, or to assess criminal activity. A guardian *ad litem* may be appointed to assess the parenting strengths and weaknesses of each parent. Once the guardian *ad litem* completes his or her investigation, he or she will make either an oral or written report to the court, or both. The court will then use this report in determining an appropriate parenting plan for the children.

8.21 What other experts may be appointed by the court in a child custody case?

If custody is disputed or if the court has concerns about a particular parent, the court may order that an expert be appointed such as a counselor to conduct a bonding assessment. In a bonding assessment, the counselor determines the strength of the child's attachment to each parent. The counselor's report is then considered by the judge.

The court may require a parent to undergo a psychological examination. This may occur where a court has concerns about potential sexual abuse or the mental functioning of one of the parents. A court may also require a parent to undergo a drug or alcohol evaluation. In all of these cases, the reports are made available to the judge for review. They are all factors the court considers when determining a parenting plan that meets the best interests of the child.

8.22 How might photographs or a video of my child help my custody case?

Photographs or a video depicting your child's day-to-day life can help the judge learn more about your child's needs. It can demonstrate how your child interacts with you, with siblings, and with other important people in your family's life. The photographs or video can portray your child's room, home, and neighborhood, as well as show your child participating in activities.

Talk to your attorney about whether photographs or a video would be helpful in your case. Photographs or video taken before the action was filed are often the most helpful. Courts are justifiably concerned that photographs or video taken after the divorce has been filed are staged or manipulated.

8.23 How might photographs, a video, or social media posts hurt my case?

By now, almost everyone has heard the stories of potential employers searching Facebook and other social media outlets, looking for information on a prospective employee. Discovery of negative information, such as partying, inappropriate behavior in public, drug use, and similar misconduct has been known to prevent the employee from being hired.

Similarly, attorneys and their clients have now turned to social media to look for evidence of misconduct by a parent. Photographs, videos, text messages, or other posts contained on these sites that show you using drugs or alcohol, or engaging in inappropriate conduct, can be used as evidence against you in your custody case. This is especially true if a court has placed restrictions on you during your case, such as no alcohol use, no exposure of your children to boyfriends or girlfriends, or other similar restrictions designed to protect your children. Information found on your social media sites, or those of your friends, can have a huge impact on your custody result. It is always best to ensure social media posts are professional and appropriate in nature.

8.24 Why might I not be awarded custody?

You may not be awarded custody if the judge determines it is in your child's best interests that custody be awarded to the other parent. A decision by the judge that your spouse should have custody does not necessarily require a conclusion that you are an unfit parent. Even if the judge determines you and your spouse are both fit to have custody, he or she may nevertheless decide it is in the best interests of your child that only one of you be awarded custody.

In determining custody and parenting arrangements, the court considers the best interests of the minor child, which include, but are not limited to the following considerations:

- The relationship of the minor child to each parent prior to the commencement of the action or the temporary hearing
- Which parent has taken greater responsibility for the day to day care of the child

- The desires and wishes of the minor child, if of an appropriate age, when such desires and wishes are based on sound reasoning
- The general health, welfare, and social behavior of the minor child
- Credible evidence of abuse inflicted on any family or household member

8.25 What does it mean to be an *unfit* parent?

Parental *unfitness* means you have a personal deficiency or incapacity which will likely prevent you from performing essential parental obligations and is likely to result in a detriment to your child's well-being. Determinations of your fitness to be a custodial parent will largely depend upon the facts of your case. Reasons why a parent might be found to be unfit include a history of domestic violence; physical, sexual or emotional abuse; alcohol or drug abuse; criminal history; sexual conduct in front of the child; or mental health problems that affect the ability to parent.

8.26 If I am awarded joint custody, what are some examples of how the parenting time might be shared?

In joint custody arrangements, many parents follow a 2-2-3 schedule, or a variation thereof, whereby one parent has the child for two weekdays, the other parent has the child for the following two weekdays, and then the child goes back to the first parent for a three-day weekend. Below is an example parenting chart to demonstrate the 2-2-3 schedule.

	Monday	Tuesday	Wednesday	Thursday	Friday	Saturday	Sunday
Week 1	Mother at 8 A.M.	Mother	Father Beginning at 5:00 P.M.	Father	Mother Beginning at 5:00 P.M.	Mother	Mother
Week 2	Father at 8 A.M.	Father	Mother Beginning at 5:00 P.M.	Mother	Father Beginning at 5:00 P.M.	Father	Father

Some parents prefer to have a one-week-on, one-week-off parenting schedule. However, the drawback to this schedule is that the child is away from the other parent for such an extended period of time. A counselor can often offer helpful insight as to which parenting plan is best for your children.

8.27 Does joint custody always mean equal time at each parent's house?

Yes. Joint custody means that each parent has equal parenting time.

8.28 How is the "decision-making" section of a parenting plan decided?

The parents, or the court, will decide who has decision-making authority. This is a specific section of the parenting plan. The three most typical areas of major decision making are religious upbringing, nonemergency medical treatment, and education. Some parenting plans also include major decision-making issues such as day care and extracurricular activities, but these are less typical. The court can award either sole or joint decision making in these major decision areas.

If you are awarded sole decision-making authority, you have the sole authority to make fundamental decisions for your child such as what school your child will attend, who will be your child's treating physician, whether your child should undergo elective treatments or surgeries, and where your child will be baptized. A parent will typically be awarded sole decision-making authority where the other parent is unavailable due to geographic distance or where the other parent has a history which includes any of the following: domestic violence; physical, sexual or emotional abuse; alcohol or drug abuse; criminal history; sexual conduct in front of the child; or mental health problems which affect the ability to parent.

If you are awarded joint decision making, you and your spouse will share the decision-making authority. Most parenting plans have joint decision making ordered. The ability to communicate between spouses is a necessity. If you share joint decision making and are unable to reach agreement on a major decision, such as a child's school or child-care provider, you and your former spouse may be required to return to mediation or to court to resolve your dispute.

8.29 If my spouse is awarded custody of our child, how much time will our child spend with me?

Parenting time schedules for noncustodial parents vary from case to case. However, the standard parenting time schedule for noncustodial parents is alternating weekends and one evening during the week. The midweek visit may be an overnight visit. Similarly, the weekends may extend to Monday morning when the parent takes the child to school. Additionally, holidays are alternated between the parents. For example, Mother's Day and Father's Day are spent with the appropriate parent, and the child's birthdays are alternated. School vacations (spring, winter and summer) are usually shared in some manner.

As in the determination of custody, the best interests of the child are what a court considers in determining the parenting time schedule. Among factors which can impact a parenting time schedule is the past history of parenting time, the age and needs of the child, and the parents' work schedules. The court works to ensure the child is stable and comfortable in both parents' residences.

8.30 What is a *parenting plan?*

A *parenting plan* is a document detailing how you and your spouse will parent your child after the divorce. Among the issues addressed in a parenting plan are:

- Custody
- Parenting time, including specific times for:
    * Regular school year
    * Holidays
    * Birthdays
    * Mother's Day and Father's Day
    * Summer, spring, and winter breaks
- Phone access to the child
- Communication regarding the child
- Access to records regarding the child
- Notice regarding parenting time
- Attendance at the child's activities

112

- Decision making regarding the child
- Exchange of information such as addresses, phone numbers, and care providers
- Relocation of the custodial parent

A detailed parenting plan is good for children and parents. It increases clarity for the parents, provides security for the child in knowing what to expect, reduces conflict, and lowers the risk of needing to return to court for a modification of your divorce decree. You should seek to have a parenting plan entered as soon as is reasonably possible after beginning the divorce process. Please see the sample parenting plan contained in the Appendix.

8.31 I don't think it's safe for my children to have any contact with my spouse. How can I prove this to the judge?

Keeping your children safe is of such importance that this discussion with your attorney requires immediate attention. Talk with your attorney immediately about a plan for the protection of you and your children. Options include a protection order, supervised visitation, or certain restrictions on your spouse's parenting time, such as no overnight visitation.

Give your attorney a complete history of the facts upon which you base the belief that your children are not safe with the other parent. Although the most recent facts are often the most relevant, it is important that your attorney to have a clear picture of the background.

Your attorney also needs information about your spouse, such as whether your spouse is or has been:

- Using alcohol or drugs or involved in the sales of such
- Treated for alcohol or drug use
- Arrested, charged, or convicted of crimes of violence or other serious crimes
- Suicidal, seriously depressed, or having other serious mental health disorders
- Subject to a protection order for harassment or violence

- Involved in pornography or other sexual misconduct around the children

8.32 How can I get my spouse's parenting time to be supervised?

If you are concerned about the safety of your children when they're with your spouse, talk to your attorney immediately. A protection order may be warranted under the circumstances to terminate or limit contact between your spouse and your children. Alternatively, it is possible to ask the judge to consider certain court orders intended to better protect your children.

Ask your attorney whether, under the facts of your case, the judge would consider any of the following court orders:

- Supervised visits
- Exchanges of the children in a public place
- Parenting class for the other parent
- Anger management or other rehabilitative program for the other parent
- A prohibition against drinking or non-prescribed drug use by the other parent when with the children

Judges have differing approaches to cases where children are at risk. Recognize there are also practical considerations, such as cost or the availability of people to supervise visits. Urge your attorney to advocate zealously for court orders to protect your children from harm by the other parent.

8.33 My spouse keeps saying he will get custody because there were no witnesses to his abuse and I can't prove it. Is he right?

No. Most domestic violence is not witnessed by others, and judges know this. If you have been a victim of abusive behavior by your spouse, or if you have witnessed your children as victims, your testimony is likely to be the most compelling evidence.

Be sure to tell your attorney about anyone who may have either seen your spouse's behavior or spoken to you or your children right after an abusive incident. They may be important witnesses in your custody case. Also, your attorney may have ideas you have not thought of for presenting persuasive evidence to the court. You should not fear, nor cater to, your spouse's threats.

8.34 I am concerned about protecting my child from abuse by my spouse. Which types of past abuse by my spouse are important to tell my attorney?

Keeping your child safe is your top priority. For your attorney to help you protect your child, provide a full history of the following:

- Hitting, kicking, pushing, shoving, or slapping your or your child
- Sexual abuse
- Threats to harm you or the child
- Threats to abduct your child
- Destruction of property
- Torture or harm to pets
- Requiring your child to keep secrets

The process of writing down past events may help you to remember other incidents of abuse you had forgotten. Be as complete as possible.

8.35 What documents or items should I give my attorney to help prove the history of domestic violence by my spouse?

The following may be useful exhibits if your case goes to court:

- Photographs of injuries
- Photographs of damaged property
- Abusive or threatening notes, letters, texts, or e-mails
- Abusive or threatening voice messages
- Your journal entries about abuse
- Police reports
- Medical records
- Court records
- Criminal records
- Damaged property, such as torn clothing

115

- Records from your counselor or clergy

Tell your attorney which of these you have or are able to obtain. Ask your attorney whether others can be acquired through a subpoena or other means.

8.36 I want to talk to my spouse about our child, but all she wants to do is argue. How can I communicate without it always turning into a fight?

Because conflict is high between you and your spouse, consider the following:

- Ask your attorney to help obtain a court order for custody and parenting time that is specific and detailed. A quality parenting plan lowers the amount of necessary communication between you and your spouse.

- Put as much information in writing as possible.

- Consider using e-mail or mail, especially for less urgent communication.

- Avoid criticisms of your spouse's parenting.

- Avoid telling your spouse how to parent.

- Be factual and business-like.

- Acknowledge to your spouse the good parental qualities he or she displays, such as being concerned, attentive, or generous.

- Keep your child out of any conflicts.

By focusing on your behavior, conflict with your spouse has the potential to decrease. Additionally, talk to your attorney about developing a communication protocol to follow when communicating with your spouse. Unfortunately, in some cases, no contact or minimal contact might be necessary.

8.37 What if the child is not returned from parenting time at the agreed-upon time? Should I call the police?

Calling the police should be done only as a last resort if you feel your child is at risk of abuse or neglect, or if you have been advised by your attorney that such a call is warranted. The involvement of law enforcement officials in parental conflict can result in far greater trauma to a child than a late return at the end of a parenting time. Further, law enforcement will ordinarily not get involved in parenting disputes.

The appropriate response to a child not being returned according to a court order depends upon the circumstances. Generally, you should consider filing a motion for contempt. In a contempt proceeding, the judge will order appropriate sanctions if she finds that the plan was violated in bad faith and without reasonable excuse. If the problem is recurring, talk with your attorney about changing the parenting schedule to eliminate these problems. Regardless of the behavior of the other parent, make every effort to keep your child out of any conflicts.

8.38   If I have custody, may I move out of state without the permission of the court?

No. A custodial parent must obtain permission of the court prior to moving out of state with a child. Permission is needed even if you are only moving out of the child's school district. You must give your former spouse notice of the relocation in a way that complies with Washington's relocation statute. A copy of the pertinent portions of the statute is contained in your parenting plan. If your plan is too old to contain these relocation provisions, call your attorney.

If your former spouse agrees to your move, contact your attorney for preparing and submitting the necessary documents to your former spouse and the court for approval. If your former spouse objects to your move, you must apply to the court for permission, give your spouse notice of your motion to relocate, and have a court hearing for the judge to decide. If you move without the court's permission, you can be found in contempt of court and restraining orders against you may be issued by the court.

To obtain the court's permission, you must first prove you have a legitimate reason for the move, such as a better job or a transfer of your new spouse's employment. You must also prove the move is in the best interests of your child. You can ask the court for temporary relocation of a child if you need to move before the final trial.

8.39 I am considering moving out of state. What factors will the court consider in either granting or denying my request to remove my child from Washington?

If you are considering an out-of-state move, talk to your attorney immediately. In order to leave Washington with your child, you must have a legitimate reason for leaving the state, such as an increased employment opportunity, education necessities, or similar good-faith reasons. The move must also be deemed by the court to be in your child's best interests. In determining your child's best interests, the court may consider many factors, including: the potential the move holds for increasing your child's quality of life; the extent to which your income or employment will be enhanced; the new living conditions and educational advantages in your new state; the relationship between your child and each parent; and your child's ties to Washington.

The court will also consider the impact the move will have on contact between your child and the other parent. Before you finalize your plans to leave Washington, seek advice from your attorney. He or she can help gather important and necessary information for your relocation case. A request to relocate should be considered carefully and good legal advice is crucial.

8.40 After the divorce, can my spouse legally take our children out of the state or out of the country during parenting time?

It depends upon the terms of the court order as set forth in your parenting plan. In most cases, the courts do not have a problem with travel between states. This is especially true for short trips across state lines. If the other parent wishes to travel to a foreign country with your child, the court will look at the circumstances surrounding this travel much more closely.

The court is more likely to restrict foreign travel if the other parent has parental conduct issues or if the judge feels that the travel would not be safe. If you are concerned about your children being out of Washington with the other parent, you may want some of these decree provisions regarding out-of-state or foreign travel with your child:

- Limits on the duration or distance for out-of-state travel with the child

- Notice requirements
- Information on phone numbers
- Information on physical addresses
- E-mail address contact information
- Possession of the child's passport
- Requiring a court order for travel outside the country

8.41 If I am not given custody, what rights do I have regarding medical records and medical treatment for my child?

Regardless of which parent has custody, joint medical decision making allows both parents access to the medical records of their children and to make emergency medical decisions. Ask your attorney to add this language to your parenting plan. It can be of assistance in dealing with care providers who are reluctant to provide you full access.

8.42 If I'm not the custodial parent, how will I know what's going on at my child's school? What rights do I have to records?

Regardless of your custodial status, if you have joint educational decision-making, you have a right to have access to your child's school records and be involved in educational decisions that affect your child. You may be provided access even if the other parent has sole educational decision-making authority. Ask your attorney to have education language inserted into your parenting plan. It can be of assistance in dealing with school administrators who are reluctant to provide you full access.

Develop a relationship with your child's teachers and the school staff. Request to be put on the school's mailing list for all notices. Find out what is necessary for you to get copies of important school information and report cards. Unless your parenting plan provides otherwise, you should be able to visit your child's class, volunteer in-class or on field trips, and attend your child's school-related events.

Communicate with the other parent to both share and receive information about your child's progress in school. This will enable you to support your child, and one another, through any challenging periods of your child's education. It also enables you to share a mutual pride in your child's successes. Regardless of which parent has custody, your child will benefit by both parents being involved in his or her education.

8.43 If my spouse is awarded custody, can I still take my child to church during my parenting time?

Yes. The noncustodial parent retains the authority to make day-to-day decisions for the child while he or she is in their care. This means that a noncustodial parent can still take their child to church or participate in religious activities during their parenting time. The court will only become involved if the particular religious activity is so different from how the child was raised that it causes trauma to the child.

8.44 What if my child does not want to visit the other parent? Can my former spouse force the child to go?

If your child resists going with the other parent, it can first be helpful to determine the underlying reason. Consider these questions:

- What is your child's stated reason for not wanting to go?

- Does your child appear afraid, anxious, or sad?

- Do you have any concerns regarding your child's safety while with the other parent?

- Have you prepared your child for being with the other parent, speaking about the experience with enthusiasm and encouragement?

- Is it possible your child perceives your anxiety about the situation and is consequently having the same reaction?

- Have you provided support for your child's transition to the other home, such as completing fun activities in your home well in advance of the other parent's starting time?

- Have you spoken to the other parent about your child's behavior?

- Can you provide anything to ensure your child's time with the other parent is comfortable, such as a favorite toy or blanket?

- Have you established clear routines that support your child to be ready to go with the other parent with ease, such as packing a backpack or saying good-bye to a family pet?

The reason for a child's reluctance to go with the other parent may be as simple as being sad about leaving you or as serious as being a victim of abuse in the other parent's home. It is important to look at this closely to determine the best response. However, it is equally important to follow a lawful order of the court.

Judges treat compliance with court orders for parenting time seriously. If one parent believes that the other is intentionally interfering with parenting time or the parent-child relationship, it can result in further litigation and you face being in contempt of court. Repeat violations can even lead to imprisonment or loss of custody. Unless you believe your child is at immediate risk, always follow the parenting plan. If the problem is ongoing, talk with your attorney about getting a counselor involved or changing the parenting plan.

9

Child Support

Whether you will be receiving or paying, child support is often the subject of much worry. Will you receive enough support to take care of your children? Will you have enough money to live on after you pay child support? How will you make ends meet?

Most parents want to provide for their children. Today, child-support laws make it possible for parents to have a better understanding of the obligation to support their children. The mechanisms for both payment and receipt of child support are more clearly defined, and help is available for collecting support if it is not paid. The *Washington Child Support Guidelines*, the *Division of Child Support (DCS)*, and your child-support enforcement officer all help simplify the child-support system. As you learn more about it, matters regarding child support that appear complex in the beginning eventually become routine for you and the other parent.

9.1   What determines whether I will get child support?

The custodial parent receives child support. The noncustodial parent will not receive child support regardless of his or her financial circumstances. Child support may also be available when there is a joint custody and one parent earns less than the other.

9.2 Can I get temporary support while waiting for custody to be decided?

Yes. A judge has the authority to enter a temporary order for custody and child support. This order ordinarily remains in place until a final decree establishing custody is entered. In most cases a hearing for temporary custody and support can be held shortly after the filing of the petition for dissolution.

If you are in need of temporary support, talk to your attorney at the first opportunity. If an agreement is not reached with your spouse, it is likely that your attorney will file a motion for temporary support, asking the judge to decide how much the support should be and when it will start. Because there are a number of steps to getting a temporary child-support order, do not delay in discussing your need for support with your attorney. Child support will not be ordered for any period prior to the filing of the petition for dissolution.

The following are the common steps in the process:

- You discuss your need for temporary child support with your attorney.

- Your attorney requests a hearing date from the judge and prepares the necessary motion for temporary order documents.

- A temporary orders hearing is held.

- The temporary order is signed by the judge.

- Your spouse's employer is notified to begin withholding your support from your spouse's paychecks.

- Your spouse's employer sends the support to the Division of Child Support (DCS).

- DCS sends the money to you.

If your spouse is not paying you support voluntarily, time is of the essence in obtaining a temporary order for support. This should be one of the first issues you discuss with your attorney.

9.3 How soon does my spouse have to start paying support for the children?

Your spouse may begin paying you support voluntarily at any time. A temporary order for support will give you the right to collect the support if your spouse is unwilling to pay any amount, is unwilling to pay the amount required by the state support schedules, or stops paying altogether. Talk to your attorney about court hearings for temporary support in your county. It is best to get the support order in place as soon as is reasonably possible. You may have to wait a week or two before your temporary hearing. It is possible that the judge will not order child support to start until the first of the following month.

9.4 How is the amount of child support that I will receive, or that I will pay, calculated?

The Washington State Child Support Guidelines were created by the state legislature to set forth the standards by which your child support is calculated. According to the guidelines, both parents have a duty to contribute to the support of their children in proportion to their respective net incomes. As a result, both your income and the income of your spouse factor into the child-support calculation.

Other factors the court may consider include:

- Substantial fluctuations of annual earnings by either parent during prior years
- The additional cost of health insurance for the children
- The amount of contributions to certain retirement plans
- Union dues or other mandatory deductions

A court may deviate from child-support guidelines, and order an amount of support different from the guideline amount. A court may deviate in these instances:

- When a parent is below the need standard
- When a parent has substantial debt not voluntarily incurred
- When a child has extraordinary medical costs or extracurricular expenses

124

- When a child is disabled and/or has special needs
- When a parent has income that exceeds the support guidelines or other indicia of substantial wealth
- The existence of children from other relationships and/or child support regularly paid for other children
- The amount of parenting time exercised by the noncustodial parent

Due to the complexity of calculations under the guidelines, most family law judges use computer software to calculate child support.

9.5 Will the type of custody arrangement or the amount of parenting time I have impact the amount of child support that I receive or that I pay?

It can. The court can lower child support if the noncustodial parent is awarded substantial parenting time in the parenting plan. The closer a noncustodial parent gets to having 50 percent of the parenting time, the more likely it is that a judge may lower the child support to be paid. This is commonly known as a *residential credit* of a *child-support deviation*. This type of deviation is *discretionary*, meaning that the judge does not have to grant it. A judge will typically not grant the deviation if it leaves the custodial parent with insufficient money to meet family needs. The use of a residential credit or deviation varies widely throughout the state. For this reason, it is essential that you discuss child support with your attorney.

9.6 Is overtime pay considered in the calculation of child support?

Yes, overtime pay is considered by the court if it is a routine part of your employment you expect to earn regularly. The judge considers your work history, the degree of control you have over your overtime, and the field in which you work. The court may decide to not include overtime if it is being incurred in order to meet certain qualifying obligations or to pay down certain debt, or if it is sporadic and undependable.

9.7 Will rental income be factored into my child support?

Yes. Income from other sources will be considered by the court in determining the amount of child support.

9.8 My spouse has a college degree but refuses to get a job. Will the court consider this in determining the amount of child support?

The court will consider the spouse's educational background and his or her earning capacity. The court can also look at your spouse's work history, health, and need for job retraining. If the court finds a spouse is voluntarily unemployed or underemployed, the court can set income for the spouse at a level the spouse should be earning. This action is known as an *imputation.* If you believe your spouse is earning substantially less than the income she or he is capable of earning, provide your attorney with details. Ask about making a case for child support based on an imputation of income.

9.9 Will I get the child support directly from my spouse or from the state?

Washington law permits either option. In the vast majority of cases however, child support is withheld by the state from the income of the spouse paying child support. Employers routinely withhold child support from employee wages just as they withhold taxes or retirement monies. If the parent receiving child support wants state collection, the court will usually order it.

There are good reasons for both spouses to have child support withheld by the state. For the spouse receiving child support, it means that support will be dependable rather than hoping for a check to arrive in the mail from a spouse who may not desire to pay the amount ordered. For the spouse paying child support, it means an accurate record is kept of the support being paid. Without an accurate record, a paying spouse can be subjected to contempt of court proceedings, judgments, and can even be forced to repay the support if he or she cannot prove payment.

9.10 How will I receive my child-support payment?

If you have selected wage withholding by the state, the Washington Division of Child Support (DCS) will disburse your child-support money. Disbursement typically occurs within three to five business days. Contact your DCS caseworker for further information. This information is readily available online and a phone number will be included in your child-support order.

If you elect to receive payments directly from your spouse you will typically receive a payment in the mail. Some spouses agree to direct deposits into bank accounts. On rare occasions, a spouse may personally deliver the support, but this kind of payment is frowned upon due to the potential for conflict.

9.11 Is there any reason not to pay or receive payments directly to or from my spouse once the court has entered a child-support order?

Yes. Once a child-support order is entered by the court, the Washington Division of Child Support (DCS) keeps a record of all support paid. If the payment is not made through DCS, the state's records will show you as behind in child-support payments. If a parent falls behind on payment, DCS has the authority to take other collection action such as additional wage withholding, income tax refund withholding, liens, driver's license suspension, and other remedies. These remedies are not available in direct payment situations.

Direct payments of child support can also result in misunderstandings between parents. The paying parent may have intended the money to be a child-support payment, while the receiving parent thought it was extra money to help with the child's expenses. If the intent was not clear, some payments could be deemed a gift by the court. Further, there may be no record of payments in cash or money order situations. The paying parent can be liable for support payments for up to ten years. Few people keep these types of records and in the event of a dispute, a parent may be left repaying support for which no record exists. The payment of support through DCS protects both parents.

9.12 Can I go to the courthouse to pick up my child-support payment?

No. Child support is not processed through the courts.

9.13 How soon can I expect my child-support payments to start arriving?

A number of factors affect the date on which you will begin receiving child support. The following are the usual steps in the process:

- A child-support amount and start date for the support is decided either by agreement between you and your spouse or by the judge.

- Either your attorney or your spouse's attorney prepares the court order.

- The attorney who did not write the court order reviews and approves it.

- The court order is taken to the judge for signature.

- The order either requires DCS to withhold support or it allows for direct payment.

- Your spouse's employer withholds the support from the paycheck, or you will receive a check directly from your spouse.

- For wage-withholding cases, the child support is transferred by the employer to the DCS payment center.

- DCS sends the money to you.

This process includes many steps. Plan your budget knowing the initial payment of child support may be delayed. For this reason, attorneys often have the spouse paying support send the payment directly to the other parent for the first two months. After that, wage withholding begins from the state. Once a parent is in the DCS system, payment is received by the parent three to five days after DCS receives payment from the employer.

9.14 Will some amount of child support be taken from every paycheck?

It depends upon how your child support order is written and also upon how DCS has issued its *wage-withholding order.* This order tells the employer how much and how often child support should be taken from a paycheck. It is common for a portion of child support to be taken from every paycheck. However, a child-support order can direct DCS to collect the support out of the first paycheck of the month or even the last paycheck. This is not typical, though. Over time, child-support payments generally fall into a routine schedule, which makes it easier for both the parent paying support and the parent receiving support to plan their budgets.

9.15 If my spouse has income other than from an employer, is it still possible to get a court order to withhold my child support from his income?

Yes. Child support can be automatically withheld from most sources of income. These may include unemployment, worker's compensation, retirement plans, and other income sources.

9.16 Can I collect child support from both the biological parent and the adoptive parent of my child?

When your child was adopted, the biological parent's duty to support the child ended. However, it may be possible for you to collect past=due child support from the period of time before the adoption.

9.17 What happens with child support when our children go to other parent's home for summer vacation? Is child support still due?

Whether child support is adjusted during extended parenting times with the noncustodial parent depends upon the court order in your case. Most often, the court does not make adjustments for residential time that occurs during school breaks. Before your divorce decree is entered by the court, talk with your attorney about receiving a child-support reduction if you anticipate having the child for an extended portion of the summer.

9.18   After the divorce, if I choose to live with my new partner or remarry, can I still collect child support?

Yes. Although spousal maintenance may end if you live with your partner or remarry, child support does not terminate for this reason.

9.19   Can I still collect child support if I move to another state?

Yes. An out-of-state move will not end your right to receive child support.

9.20   How long can I expect to receive child support?

Generally, child support is ordered to be paid until the child graduates from high school or turns eighteen, whichever occurs later. Exceptions to this general rule include cases involving a child with special needs or orders terminating child support at age eighteen. Washington also allows for support during college under certain circumstances. This is known as postsecondary support. All of these areas should be discussed with your attorney well before your child turns eighteen to ensure you do not run into problems in collecting support. If you miss certain deadlines required by your child-support order or as required by the law, you may be permanently barred from receiving additional support.

9.21   Does interest accrue on past-due child support?

Yes, interest accrues on past-due child support. DCS does not calculate interest for you, however. If you want to collect the interest due, you must have a judgment entered in court. Once the court enters this judgment, DCS will collect it.

9.22   What can I do if my former spouse refuses to pay child support?

If your former spouse is not paying child support, you may take action to enforce the court order with the help of your attorney, by yourself, or through the assistance of DCS. Both attorneys and private individuals can file a motion for contempt with the court. If the judge finds the parent in contempt for failing to pay child support when ordered, the judge can enter a judgment ordering interest, the payment of attorney fees, or other sanctions. A court can even order imprisonment.

A parent can also ask DCS to assist with collection. DCS can conduct wage withholding, seize tax refunds, seize bank accounts, and even suspend driver's licenses if a parent falls behind in child-support payments. DCS can seize other property and can take other collections actions as well.

9.23 At what point will the state help me collect back child support?

The state will help you collect back child support as soon as you ask it to do so. In some cases, the state will first have to send out certain notices, so there may be a short delay in services. You must initiate contact with the state if you want help in collecting your child support unless your order of child support already automatically provides for state assistance.

9.24 I live outside Washington. Will the money I spend on airline tickets to see my children be shared?

Generally, yes. Washington law provides each parent will share in appropriate long-distance transportation costs in proportion to respective net incomes. Sometimes parents make additional flights to see their children in school plays, weddings, religious ceremonies, and other special occasions. However, if these visits are not specifically provided for in the parenting plan, they may not be reimbursed.

9.25 After the divorce, can my former spouse substitute buying sprees with the child for child-support payments?

No. Purchases of gifts and clothing for a child do not relieve your former spouse from an obligation to pay child support.

9.26 Are child care expenses shared by the parents?

Yes. Work and school-related child care expenses are generally shared by the parents in proportion to their respective net incomes. There can be exceptions. For example, if a parent is using very expensive child care such as a nanny, the court may order a reduced contribution or order that less expensive services be obtained. If a parent's income leaves him or her under the poverty standard, commonly known as the *need standard,* the obligation may be reduced or eliminated. The court may restrict the ability of a family member to charge the other parent for day care without clear evidence showing the income is being claimed for tax purposes. Other exceptions may also apply.

9.27 How does providing health insurance for my child affect my child-support amount?

If you pay the health insurance premium for your child, the amount you pay is taken into account when calculating child support. You will receive a credit for the amount you pay per month for your child's health insurance premium.

9.28 Am I required to pay for my child's uninsured medical expenses?

Yes. Uninsured medical expenses are generally shared by the parents in proportion to their respective net incomes. There may be exceptions where medical care was cosmetic or unnecessary, or in certain circumstances where the other parent's consent was required but not first obtained.

9.29 Am I required to pay for general, everyday expenses for my child with the support I receive?

Yes, if you are receiving child support, under the guidelines you are responsible for such expenses as housing, clothing, school lunch, and the cost for normal activities. Work- or school-related day care, uninsured medical expenses, and long distance transportation expenses are usually shared in addition to the child support. Under certain circumstances, the court can also order the parents to share in extracurricular expenses. This more typically occurs where the costs are very high, such as with traveling sports teams, equestrian activities, or involvement in music.

9.30 Can my spouse be required by the decree to pay for our child's private elementary and high school education?

Potentially; if you can show the court the parents had a prior agreement to provide private education for the children it is more likely. This is especially true if other siblings have received private education or if the parents had a history of receiving private education. Of course, the economic circumstance of each spouse is a factor. Getting the court to order the payment of private education is far from certain. If you want your spouse to share this expense for your child, talk it over with your attorney. Be sure to provide your attorney with information regarding tuition, fees, and other expenses related to private education.

9.31 Can my spouse be required by the decree to contribute financially to our child's college education?

Yes. Washington laws do provide the potential for your child to receive postsecondary education support under certain circumstances. In order for your child to receive post-secondary support, you must request it from the court before the court loses jurisdiction over the child. This usually occurs when the child turns eighteen or graduates from high school, whichever is last. However, some orders provide for earlier termination, such as upon the child's eighteenth birthday. The postsecondary support laws are a trap for the unwary, and many attorneys who do not regularly practice in the area of family law do not fully understand them. If you fail to properly follow your court order or fail to follow the postsecondary support laws, your child could lose all rights to postsecondary support.

The only safe way to handle postsecondary support is to discuss it with your attorney when the child-support order is entered. Then, check in with your attorney as soon as your child turns seventeen, or better yet, when your child turns sixteen. Ask what steps you should take to ensure post-secondary support will be ordered. Get postsecondary support issues resolved with your attorney long before your child turns eighteen. This is not an area to navigate alone.

Assuming you have timely requested postsecondary support from the court by filing a petition for modification of child support and the required supporting documents, the judge will consider your request. A judge is not required to order postsecondary support, and orders vary from judge to judge. Judges award postsecondary support if it is warranted by the circumstances. In determining whether to award support and how much to be awarded, a judge will consider the earnings history of each spouse and the ability to pay, the aptitude of the child, the child's choice of college, the availability of financial aid, and other factors. Again, this is a complex legal area. You are dealing with a college education that usually costs tens of thousand of dollars. Do not risk this. Get help from an attorney if at all possible.

10

Spousal Maintenance

The mere mention of the term "spousal maintenance" often stirs emotions. When there does not seem to be enough money to go around, and suddenly one income is being asked to support two households, spousal maintenance may seem like an injustice to the spouse paying it. On the other hand, if you are seeking spousal maintenance, you may feel upset your spouse is resistant in helping support you. This may be especially true if you interrupted your own career to stay home and care for your children.

10.1 What's the difference between *spousal maintenance* and *alimony*?

In Washington, *spousal maintenance* and *alimony* have the same meaning. It is referred to as spousal maintenance, however, by the courts and family law attorneys.

10.2 How will I know if I am eligible to receive spousal maintenance?

In Washington, spousal maintenance is awarded on a "need and ability to pay" basis. This means one spouse must have a documented need for spousal maintenance in order to meet their monthly obligations after consideration is given to his or her monthly income, if any. The other spouse must have the ability to pay spousal maintenance after consideration is given to his or her income and reasonable monthly expenses. Judges usually see through attempts by one side to artificially increase the "need" for more maintenance, as well as efforts

135

by a spouse to increase expenses in order to escape a finding of "ability to pay." Factors that may affect your eligibility to receive spousal maintenance include:

- The length of your marriage
- Your need for education or other rehabilitation in order to find meaningful employment. This is especially true if you interrupted your career to care for your children or to support your spouse's career.
- Your work history and earning capacity
- Your health
- Your overall financial situation compared to that of your spouse, including your prospects for future earnings, especially in long-term marriages
- The lifestyle enjoyed during the marriage, especially in long-term marriages

Every case for spousal maintenance is unique. Providing your attorney with clear and detailed information about the facts of your marriage and current situation will allow him or her to make an informed spousal maintenance assessment. Your attorney must make a careful calculation of your spouse's monthly net income and available income in order to determine the "ability to pay." Similarly, a careful calculation must be made of your net income, if any, along with monthly expenses in order to determine your "need." Your attorney will typically use a form called a *financial declaration* in order to present this information to the court.

10.3   What information should I provide to my attorney if I want spousal maintenance?

If your attorney advises that you may be a candidate for spousal maintenance, be sure to provide complete facts about your situation, including:

- A history of interruptions in your education or career for the benefit of your spouse, including transfers or moves due to your spouse's employment
- A history of interruptions in your education or career for raising children, including periods during which you worked part-time

- Your complete educational background, including the dates of your schooling or training and degrees earned
- Your work history, including the names of your employers, the dates of your employment, your duties, your pay, and the reasons you left
- Any pensions or other benefits lost due to the interruption of your career for the benefit of the marriage
- Your health history, including any current diagnoses, treatments, limitations, and medications
- Your current monthly living expenses and anticipated future expenses
- A complete list of the debts of you and your spouse
- Income from all sources for you and your spouse. Document this income with personal and business tax returns and W-2s for three years, recent pay stubs, and current profit-loss statements for any businesses. This will give your attorney a good start in preparation of financial considerations.

10.4   My spouse told me because I had an affair during the marriage I have no chance to receive spousal maintenance, even though I quit my job and have cared for our children for many years. Is it true I have no case?

No. Washington is a "no-fault" state and infidelities usually have no effect on spousal maintenance. However, if your affair had a significant financial impact on the marital estate, it may be taken into consideration when determining an award of spousal maintenance.

10.5   How is the amount of spousal maintenance calculated?

Unlike child support, there are no specific guidelines for determining the amount of spousal maintenance. A judge will look at the expenses and incomes of you and your spouse, after giving consideration to the payment and receipt of child support, if applicable. Judges are given discretion to determine spousal maintenance without the benefit of specific guidelines. Consequently, the outcome of a spousal maintenance ruling by a judge can be an unpredictable aspect of your divorce.

Generally, a judge attempts to ensure each spouse has enough income to meet his or her reasonable month expenses. Sometimes this is not possible as there is not enough income to go around. Spouses will then be forced to cut expenses.

10.6 My spouse makes more money than he reports on our tax return, but he hides it. How can I prove my spouse's real income to show he can afford to pay spousal maintenance?

Alert your attorney to these concerns. Your attorney can then take a number of actions to determine your spouse's income with greater accuracy. These actions likely include:

- More thorough discovery
- An examination of check registers and bank deposits
- Inquiries about travel
- Depositions of third parties who have knowledge of income or spending by your spouse
- Subpoena of records of places where your spouse has made large purchases or received income
- Comparison of income claimed with expenses paid
- Inquiries about purchases made in cash

By partnering with your attorney, you may be able to establish your spouse's actual income as greater than is shown on tax returns. If you filed joint tax returns, discuss with your attorney any other implications of erroneous information on those returns.

10.7 I want to be sure the records on the spousal maintenance I pay are accurate, especially for tax purposes. What is the best way to ensure this occurs?

If you are paying child support in addition to spousal support, your spousal maintenance should be made to the Division of Child Support (DCS). Spousal maintenance can be automatically withheld from your pay, just like child support. By avoiding direct payments to your former spouse, you will have accurate records. To avoid an audit by the Internal Revenue Service, you must deduct the same amount of spousal maintenance your spouse is reporting as income on your tax returns.

10.8 What effect does spousal maintenance have on my taxes?

If you are required to pay spousal maintenance pursuant to a court order, your payments are tax deductible. Likewise, if you receive spousal maintenance pursuant to a court order, you must pay income tax on the amount received.

10.9 How is the purpose of spousal maintenance different from the payment of a property settlement?

Spousal maintenance and the division of property serve two distinct purposes, though many of the determining factors are the same. The purpose of spousal maintenance is to assist a spouse in meeting monthly financial obligations. It also provides for the rehabilitation of a spouse for any necessary training and education.

In contrast, the purpose of a property division is to distribute the marital assets fairly between you and your spouse. Courts generally believe a spouse should not be required to use marital assets to pay their monthly living expenses if the other spouse can meet their obligations without needing to use marital assets. Thus, maintenance serves as a "financial bridge" between the spouses.

10.10 My spouse makes a lot more money than I do. Will I be awarded spousal maintenance to make up the difference in our income?

Although the purpose of spousal maintenance is to provide support, maintenance awards are not necessarily used to equalize the incomes of the parties, except in long-term marriages or under special circumstances. Instead, maintenance may be awarded to assist the economically disadvantaged spouse for the transitional period during and after the divorce, until he or she becomes economically self-sufficient. However, a disparity in income is often one factor the judge considers when determining an award of spousal maintenance and the amount of the award. The main consideration will always be the "need" of one spouse and the "ability to pay" of the other spouse.

10.11 How long can I expect to receive spousal maintenance?

How long you will receive spousal maintenance will depend upon the facts of your case and the judge's philosophy toward maintenance. In general, the longer your marriage, the stronger your case is for a longer-term spousal maintenance award. The presence of minor children in your household is another very important factor, regardless of the length of the marriage.

You may receive only temporary spousal maintenance, or you may receive maintenance for several years. In some cases, a spouse may receive lifetime maintenance. This usually involved a very long-term marriage, spouses of advanced years, or a spouse with a medical disability. Talk to your attorney about the facts of your case to get a clearer picture of the possible outcomes in your situation.

10.12 Can remarriage affect my spousal maintenance?

Yes. Unless you and your spouse agree otherwise, your spousal maintenance will typically terminate upon your remarriage. Discuss with your attorney the possible exceptions to this general rule. Your divorce decree can be drafted to provide that spousal maintenance does not terminate upon marriage, but this is often a hotly contested issue.

10.13 Does the death of my former spouse affect my spousal maintenance?

Yes. Spousal maintenance ends upon the death of either party. If this is a concern, discuss with your attorney the possibility of including life insurance provisions in your decree in order to protect your future spousal maintenance and child support.

10.14. Do I have to keep paying spousal maintenance if my former spouse is now living with a new significant other?

Possibly. Do not stop making your maintenance payments. Instead, contact your attorney to seek a modification of the maintenance award. Maintenance may be reduced or terminated with a new court order if your former spouse is living with a new significant other.

Some decrees have provisions that maintenance will terminate in the event a spouse resides with a significant other (or remarries). This can be bargained for in the mediation or negotiation process. This can also be requested from the judge at a trial. If your decree contains this language, your maintenance will terminate in the event of cohabitation. Still, first contact your attorney to determine whether your spouse is truly cohabiting.

10.15 Can I continue to collect spousal maintenance if I move to a different state?

Yes. The duty of your former spouse to follow a court order to pay spousal maintenance does not end simply because you move to another state.

10.16 What can I do if my spouse stops paying spousal maintenance?

If your spouse stops paying maintenance, see your attorney about options for enforcing your court order. The judge may order the maintenance be taken from a source of your spouse's income. A judge can also order the payment of attorney fees, a judgment, interest on the deficient maintenance, and other sanctions.

If your spouse is intentionally refusing to pay spousal support, talk with your attorney about whether pursuing a contempt of court action would be effective. In a contempt action, your spouse may be ordered to appear in court and provide evidence explaining why support has not been paid. Possible consequences for contempt of court include a jail sentence, attorney fees, or other financial sanctions.

10.17 Can I return to court to modify spousal maintenance?

It depends. If your divorce decree provides your spousal maintenance order is "non-modifiable," then usually it cannot be modified. However, a court may not order spousal maintenance to be non-modifiable as part of a trial. A maintenance order can only be made non-modifiable if it is agreed to by the spouses as part of the negotiation or mediation process. Also, your decree may not be modified to award spousal maintenance if maintenance was not awarded in the original decree dissolving the marriage. Always talk with your attorney about your options before assuming you cannot modify your maintenance. There are potential exceptions.

Otherwise, if there has been a material change in the circumstances of either you or your spouse, you may seek to have your spousal maintenance modified. Examples include a serious illness or significant change in the employment status or the earnings of either spouse. Perhaps a spouse needs more time to complete education or training. A request to modify spousal maintenance for the purposes of seeking additional maintenance may not be filed if the time for payment of maintenance allowed under your original decree has already passed. If you think you have a basis to modify your maintenance, contact your attorney at once to be sure a timely modification request is filed with the court.

11

Division of Property

You never imagined you would face losing the house you and your spouse poured so much time and effort into building. Facing the loss of half, or more, of your retirement accounts can be daunting to say the least. During a divorce, either the spouses or judge will determine who is to take ownership of everything from the family home to the stock portfolio. Suddenly you find yourself having a strong attachment to a lamp in the family room or the painting in the hallway. Why does the coin collection suddenly take on new meaning? The division of property is often more contentious than parenting and support issues.

11.1 What system does Washington use for dividing property?

Washington law provides for a fair and equitable, but not necessarily equal, division of the property and debts acquired during your marriage. Regardless of how title is held, the court will use its discretion to divide the marital assets and debts. In many cases this may mean equal division, but as little as one-third of the assets awarded to one party and two-thirds to the other may still be considered "equitable." There are reported cases more extreme than this.

The court will consider a number of factors, including the current economic circumstances of you and your spouse and the length of the marriage. The future earnings potential and the health of the respective spouses will be significant factors. Generally, courts are more likely to employ a "50/50" split of the net asset value in short-term marriages or where the spouses' incomes are similar. They may begin to deviate from the "50/50" sharing in longer-term marriages where there is a significant difference in the earnings or economic outlook of the parties. The greater this difference, the greater the potential for a court to deviate in favor of the financially disadvantaged spouse.

11.2   What does *community property* mean?

Washington is a community property state. *Community property* is all property acquired during the marriage by the spouses. Property acquired before marriage or after separation, gifts, inheritances, and personal injury proceeds for pain and suffering are generally considered to be separate property. This can be a complex legal area and is one that you should carefully discuss with your attorney.

11.3   How is it determined who gets the house?

The first issue to be decided regarding the family home is the determination of who will retain possession of it while the divorce is pending. Later, it must be decided whether the house will be sold, or awarded to you or your spouse. Several factors to consider when determining the disposition of the home are:

- Who can afford the mortgage and expenses associated with the home
- Who has custody of the children
- Whether the house is premarital
- Whether there are other assets in the marital estate to offset the value of the home

Talk with your attorney about your options and to consider the above factors. If you and your spouse are unable to reach agreement regarding the house, the judge will decide who keeps it or whether it will be sold.

11.4   How do I determine how much our house is worth?

In a divorce, the value of your home can be determined a number of ways. You and your spouse can agree to the value of your home. You can seek advice from a local real estate agent on the approximate value of your home through a market analysis and these values can be used in negotiations or mediation. For a more authoritative valuation, you can hire a professional real estate appraiser to determine the value of your home. If your case is proceeding to trial, you will need an appraisal. Talk to your attorney to determine the best method to value your home in your divorce.

11.5 What is meant by *equity* in my home?

Equity is the difference between the value of the home and the amount owed in mortgages against the property. For example, if the first mortgage is $50,000 and the second mortgage from a home equity loan is $10,000, the total debt owed against the house is $60,000. If your home is valued at $100,000, the equity in your home is $40,000. (The $100,000 value less the $60,000 in mortgages equals $40,000 in equity.).

11.6 Should I sell the house during the divorce proceedings?

Selling your home is a big decision. To help you decide what is right for you, ask yourself these questions:

- What will be the impact on my children if the home is sold?
- Can I afford to stay in the house after the divorce?
- After the divorce, will I be willing to give the house and yard the time, money, and physical energy required for its maintenance?
- Is it necessary for me to sell the house to pay a share of the equity to my spouse, or are there other options?
- Would my life be easier if I were in a smaller or simpler home?
- Would I prefer to move closer to the support of friends and family?
- What is the state of the housing market in my community?
- What are the benefits of remaining in this house?
- Can I retain the existing mortgage or will I have to refinance?

- Will I have a higher or lower interest rate if I sell the house and buy a new one?
- Will I have the means to acquire another home?
- If I don't retain the home and my spouse asks for it, what effect will this have on my custody case?
- Will my spouse agree to the sale of the house?
- What will be the real estate commission?
- What will be the costs of preparing the house for sale?

Selling a home is more than just a legal or financial decision. Consider what is important to you in creating your life after divorce when deciding whether to sell your home. Always discuss this issue with your attorney in advance of making any decision to sell, as it can have a significant impact on many aspects of your case.

11.7   How will the equity in our house be divided?

If your home is going to be sold, the equity in the home will most likely be divided at the time of the sale, after the costs of the sale have been paid. If the home is sold before the divorce is final, the court may order that the sale proceeds be held in an attorney's trust account until the divorce is finalized and all assets can be divided at once. If the divorce is final, the proceeds will be divided as has been directed by the court once all mortgages, commissions, and closing costs have been paid.

If either you or your spouse will be awarded the house, there are a number of options for the other party in being compensated for his or her share of the equity in the marital home. These may include:

- The spouse who does not receive the house receives other assets (for example, retirement funds or stock accounts) to compensate for their respective share of the equity.
- The person who remains in the home agrees to refinance it at some future date, and to pay the other party his or her share of the equity.

- The parties agree the property will be sold at a future date, or upon the occurrence of a certain event such as the youngest child completing high school or the remarriage of the party keeping the home.

11.8 My house is worth less than what is owed. What are my options?

This may or may not be a problem for you. If you want to keep the house, you can continue to make the payments. Because you have negative equity in the home, you will actually receive additional assets to offset this negative equity. This can be a favorable situation for you, particularly if you like the home. For example, if you have $10,000.00 of negative equity in a home, the court may compensate you with an additional $10,000.00 of other assets in order to make up for the negative equity loss.

If you need to sell the home, the negative equity can become problematic. In this case, both you and your spouse will need to pay the difference between what your home is sold for and what is owed on the mortgage. This may require you to liquidate other assets to complete the sale. Another option to consider is a short sale, where the lender accepts less money for your house than you owe. At times, the negative equity is so great that the home will simply be lost to foreclosure. Seek advice from your attorney and other financial experts to determine which option is best for you.

11.9 If my spouse signs a *quitclaim deed,* does that remove his obligation to repay the mortgage?

No. A *quitclaim deed* is a legal document that transfers one person's interest in real property to another person. However, removing your spouse's name from the title of your property does not remove their obligation to repay the mortgage. To remove a spouse from the mortgage obligation, you must seek a refinance of your current mortgage. A refinance involves obtaining a new mortgage loan to pay off the existing mortgage.

11.10 Who keeps all the household goods until the decree is signed?

The court ordinarily will not make decisions about who keeps household goods on a temporary basis, unless those items are significant or the use of the items is contested. Most couples attempt to resolve these issues on their own rather than incur legal fees to dispute household goods on a temporary basis. If the parties cannot agree on the use of the property, however, the court will decide the issue if a spouse files a motion for temporary orders and requests allocation of the household goods. Typically, the court will also enter an order restraining the parties from transferring, selling, or destroying household goods during the divorce process, so that the goods remain intact and can be divided by the decree.

11.11 How can I reduce the risk of assets being hidden, transferred, or destroyed by my spouse?

Consulting with an attorney before filing for divorce can reduce the risk of assets being hidden, transferred, or destroyed by your spouse. This is especially important if your spouse has a history of destroying property, incurring substantial debt, or transferring money without your knowledge. These are among the possible actions you and your attorney can consider together:

- Placing your family heirlooms or other valuables in a safe location
- Transferring some portion of financial accounts prior to filing for divorce
- Preparing an inventory of the personal property
- Taking photographs or video of the property
- Obtaining copies of important records or statements
- Obtaining a restraining order before your spouse is served with notice of the divorce

Plans to leave the marital home should also be discussed in detail with your attorney, so any actions taken early in your case are consistent with your ultimate goals. Speak candidly with your attorney about your concerns so a plan can be developed that provides a level of protection appropriate to your circumstances.

11.12 How are assets such as cars, boats, and furniture divided, and when does this happen?

In most cases, spouses are able to reach their own agreements about how to divide personal property, such as household furnishings and vehicles. Personal property is often awarded to the spouse who typically uses it. If you and your spouse disagree about how to divide certain items, it can be wise to consider which are truly valuable to you, financially or otherwise. Perhaps some can be easily replaced. Always look to see whether it is a good use of your attorney fees to argue over items of personal property.

If a negotiated settlement cannot be reached, the determination of how your property will be divided will be made by the judge. Prior to trial, disputes over the interim use of this property will be resolved by the court at a temporary orders hearing. At trial, the judge will make a final division of all vehicles and household goods.

11.13 How do I value our used personal property?

In a divorce, your personal property will be valued at its fair market value. The fair market value is the price a buyer would be willing to pay for the item at a garage sale or on an online auction website. For example, if you bought a sofa for $3,000 five years ago, the fair market value of the couch is what you could sell it for at a garage sale today. The fair market value is not how much the couch cost when you bought it or how much it will cost to replace the couch. Instead, the value of your personal property is what you could reasonably sell it for in its current used condition.

Spouses can usually agree on the values. If the spouses cannot agree, it is wise to have the property appraised. This will usually be a far cheaper process than taking hours of the court's time (and using your attorney fees) to testify as to what you think each item of property is worth.

11.14 My spouse and I own a collection. How will our collection be valued and divided in our divorce?

If you own a unique collection, such as a gun, art, or coin collection, talk with your attorney about how to value the collection in your divorce. Usually, you will need the collection appraised by an expert who has specialized training and knowledge to determine its value. If you and your spouse cannot agree on who will keep the collection, the judge will decide who receives it. Usually, the judge tries to place the collection with the spouse who collected it or to whom it has the most sentimental value. The judge may split the collection between each spouse. If neither spouse wants the collection, it is possible the judge will order the collection to be sold.

11.15 What is meant by a *property inventory* and how detailed should mine be?

A *property inventory* is a listing of the property you own. It may also include a brief description of the property. Discuss with your attorney the level of inventory detail needed to benefit your case. Factors to consider when creating your inventory may include:

- The extent to which you anticipate you and your spouse will disagree regarding the division of property

- Whether you anticipate a dispute regarding the value of the property either spouse is retaining

- Whether you will have continued access to the property if a later inventory is needed or whether you spouse will retain control of the property

- Whether you or your spouse are likely to disagree about which items are premarital, inherited, or gifts from someone other than your spouse

In addition to creating an inventory, your attorney may request that you prepare a list of the property you and your spouse have already divided, or a list of the items you want but your spouse has not agreed to give to you. If you do not have continued access to your property, talk to your attorney about taking photographs or obtaining access to the property to complete your inventory.

Division of Property

11.16 What happens to our individual checking and savings accounts during and after the divorce?

Regardless of whose name is on the account, bank accounts may be considered marital assets and may be divided by the court. Discuss with your attorney the benefits of a temporary restraining order to protect bank accounts, how to retain access or obtain an accounting of these accounts, and how to use these accounts while the case is pending. Usually, joint accounts will be closed, the balances divided between the spouses, and each spouse will open new accounts in their name. Accounts will sometimes be left open to pay debts that are automatically debited from the account each month, but it is wise to ultimately transfer these to separate accounts and close the joint accounts in an orderly manner.

11.17 How and when are liquid assets like bank accounts and stocks divided?

Talk with your attorney early in your case about the benefits of a temporary restraining order to reduce the risk of your spouse transferring money out of financial accounts or transferring other assets. In many cases, couples will agree to divide bank accounts equally at the outset of the case. However, this may not be advisable in your case. Discuss with your attorney whether you should keep an accounting of how you spend money from a joint bank account while your divorce is in progress.

Stocks are ordinarily a part of the final agreement for the division of property and debts. If you and your spouse cannot agree on how your investments should be divided, the judge will make the decision at trial. Often, stocks and mutual funds are used to equalize the value of other assets such as homes and retirement accounts.

11.18 How is pet custody determined?

As important as pets are to the owners, judges often see this as a matter that is not worthy of court time. Generally, there are other, more pressing issues such as child custody and financial management. The courts hope spouses can work pet custody out between them.

If the spouses cannot agree, the judge will make a determination. Pet custody is determined on a case-by-case basis. Factors that courts considered include:

- Who purchased the pet?
- Who provided the care and training for the pet?
- Who "uses" the pet? If this is a hunting dog, for example, this pet will ordinarily be awarded to the hunter.
- Who will best be able to meet the pet's needs?

11.19 How will our property in another state be divided?

For the purposes of dividing your assets, out-of-state property is generally treated the same as property in Washington. It is valued and divided with the rest of the marital estate. Although a Washington court cannot order a change in the title to property located in another state, a judge can order your spouse to either turn the property over to you or sign a deed or other document transferring title to you. Ordinarily, this is not a complicated issue.

11.20 How are retirement accounts divided?

Retirement accounts can be one of the most difficult issues spouses face in their property distribution process. The first thing that must be recognized is that retirement funds are "pretax" assets, meaning taxes have not yet been paid on them. Because taxes have not been paid on them yet, they are not worth the same amount as assets that have already been taxed, such as bank accounts, stocks, and mutual funds.

Retirement accounts have strict rules and laws governing when the accounts can be accessed. If you withdraw the money from the retirement account before the plan allows, you will be charged penalties for the early withdrawal in addition to facing tax consequences. Thus, a $100,000 retirement account is probably worth only about $72,000 today once penalties and taxes are considered.

Valuing retirement interests is a very complex process. There are two types of retirement accounts, known as a *defined benefit plan* and a *defined contribution plan*. Pension plans are referred to as "defined benefit plans," and include military and state retirements, as well as many other private retirement plans. A *defined benefit plan* means the plan holder is paid a monthly monetary benefit that begins on a set date.

There are three ways to divide a pension plan (defined benefit plan). The simplest method is to award each spouse his or her own retirements. If the amounts are the same, you are done. If the amounts are different, the difference in the retirements can be equalized with other funds. When equalizing retirements, be careful to remember retirement accounts are worth less than non-retirement funds.

The second way to divide a pension plan is to use a *Qualified Domestic Relations Order,* commonly called a *QDRO.* A QDRO is a court order telling the retirement plan administrator how to divide the plan between the spouses. A QDRO is a complicated document and should always be prepared by a qualified attorney or accountant.

The third way to divide a pension is to value it and then offset it with other property. Valuing a future pension plan benefit is known as a *present value calculation.* It is a calculation generally undertaken only by accountants and attorneys experienced in this area. Although present value calculators are readily available on the Internet, these internet calculators should only be used as a reference. Seek qualified legal help to perform this calculation.

The second type of retirement is the *defined contribution plan.* A defined contribution plan simply means the plan has a lump-sum value. With these types of plans, you usually receive a monthly or quarterly statement telling you the account's worth. These plans are commonly known as 401(k), IRA, or deferred compensation plans. Because the values are readily available and known, This type of retirement account is more easily divided.

While the simplest way to divide a defined contribution plan is to award each spouse his or her own retirements; dividing the account between the spouses is not a difficult proposition. A form from the plan administrator, or a QDRO, can be used to divide these defined contribution plans where necessary. These plans can also be equalized with other funds. Again, when equalizing retirements, always remember that retirement accounts are worth less than other non-retirement funds. Always seek the assistance of an attorney when dividing even simple plans like defined contribution plans.

11.21 What happens with Social Security, railroad Tier I retirements, or military disability retirement accounts? Can these accounts actually be divided?

This is an exceptionally complex area of law that challenges veteran family law attorneys and even judges. Disputes over the proper application of the law in this area have reached the Washington Supreme Court. Get legal help from a highly experienced divorce attorney if you are facing these issues.

Generally, Social Security benefits, railroad Tier I benefits, and military disability pay are nondivisible under federal law. This means your judge cannot award you part of your spouse's Social Security, railroad Tier I, or military disability benefit. However, the judge can compensate you for your share of these benefits from other marital assets. While the judge can compensate, it is not required. This means the judge has discretion to make an equitable award. You need help from an attorney to properly present these issues before your assigned judge.

11.22 Does each one of our financial accounts have to be divided in half if we agree to an equal division of our assets?

No. Rather than incurring the administrative challenges and expense of dividing each asset in half, you and your spouse can decide that one of you will take certain assets equal to the value of the assets taken by the other spouse. If necessary, one of you can agree to make a cash payment to the other to make an equitable division. This is known as a *property equalization payment*.

11.23 Are all of the assets that I had prior to my marriage still going to be mine after the divorce?

Assets that a party owned before the marriage are known as *separate property*. Inheritances, gifts, and personal injury proceeds for pain and suffering are also separate property. In most cases the court will allow a party to retain an asset brought into the marriage, or received through inheritance or gift. However, Washington law allows a judge to "invade" the separate assets of one spouse and award them to the other if it is necessary to make an equitable division of property. While rare for a court to do so, the following are questions the court will consider in making its determination:

- Can the premarital asset be clearly traced? For example, if you continue to own a vehicle you brought into the marriage, it is likely it will be awarded to you as your separate property. However, if you brought a vehicle into the marriage, sold it during the marriage, and then spent the proceeds, it is less likely that the court will consider awarding you its value.

- Did you keep the property separate and titled in your name, or did you commingle it with marital assets? Premarital assets you kept separate may be more likely to be awarded to you.

- Did the other spouse contribute to the increase in the value of the premarital asset, and can the value of that increase be proven? For example, suppose a woman owned a home prior to her marriage. After the marriage, the parties live in the home, continuing to make mortgage payments and improvements to the home. At the time of the divorce, the husband seeks a portion of the equity in the home. The court might consider the value of the home at the time of the marriage, any contributions made to increase the equity, and the evidence of those contributions. Payment to the other spouse for the value of these improvements or increased equity is known as an *equitable right of reimbursement*.

11.24 What does it mean to *commingle* property?

Commingling occurs when one spouse's separate property is mixed or combined with the marital property, such that the separate property can no longer be distinguished from the marital property. The commingling of bank accounts is a common example. Suppose a spouse inherited $100,000 from a parent. This is the spouse's separate property because it is an inheritance. However, also suppose that the spouse placed this

$100,000 in the joint checking account of the spouses. Then for years, the spouses put their paychecks into this account and made various withdrawals and deposits. The bank account has become so mixed it is deemed commingled.

If an account has been commingled, it is changed from a separate account to a community account and can be divided by the court as community property. However, even if this has occurred, all hope is not lost. Washington law allows a spouse to recover these separate funds if they can be "traced." A judge will determine if the separate funds have been sufficiently traced. If you believe you have received separate funds from premarital assets, inheritances, gifts, or personal injury proceeds, talk with your attorney about it. Your attorney can work with you to prepare a proper tracing for the court so you can be awarded these assets in your divorce.

11.25 Will I get to keep my engagement ring and wedding ring after the divorce?

Your engagement ring and wedding ring were gifted to you by your spouse. Because they were a gifts, they will be considered your separate property and they will be awarded to you without charge against the marital estate. However, if you personally added jewels to your ring after the marriage, these may not be considered a gift. The added portion can be valued and included as part of the marital estate.

11.26 What factors determine whether I can get a share of my spouse's business?

Many factors determine whether you will get a share of your spouse's business and in what form you may receive it. Factors the court will look at include:

- Whether your spouse owned the business prior to your marriage
- Your role, if any, in operating the business or increasing its value even if the business was owned before marriage by the other spouse
- Whether the business has any value after consideration of assets, liabilities, and goodwill

If you or your spouse owns a business, it is important to work with your attorney early in the case to develop a strategy for valuing the business, and making a case for how it should be treated in the division of property and debts. Business valuations are some of the most complex issues facing the attorney. Usually, there are only a few attorneys in each county who are highly experienced in business valuations. If there is a significant business at issue in your case, seek an attorney who has substantial experience in this area. This is another area in which a qualified CPA is hired to assist in the valuation process and to provide testimony at trial, if necessary.

11.27 My spouse and I have owned and run our own business together for many years. Can I be forced out of it?

Deciding what should happen with a family business when divorce occurs can be challenging. Because of the risk for future conflict between you and your spouse, the value of the business is likely to be substantially decreased if you both remain owners. Courts generally prefer one of two options. First is to award the business to one spouse and compensate the other spouse for his or her share of the value. Second is to have the business sold if neither spouse can buy out the other's interests in the business. Leaving both spouses as owners after a divorce is rarely successful in the long run. In discussing your options with your attorney, consider the following questions:

- If one spouse retains ownership of the business, are there enough other assets for the other spouse to receive a fair share of the total marital assets?

- Which spouse has the skills and experience to continue running the business?

- What would you do if you weren't working in the business?

- What is the value of the business?

- What is the market for the business if it were to be sold?

- Could you remain an employee of the business for some period of time even if you were not an owner?

You and your spouse know your business best. With the help of your attorneys and business valuation experts, you may be able to create a settlement satisfactory to you both. If not, the judge will make the decision for you at trial.

11.28 My spouse is employed in a professional capacity. Is there a value to this profession?

There may be a substantial value to your spouse's profession. A component of a professional business is a *goodwill valuation*. A goodwill valuation is often associated with doctors, dentists, attorneys, veterinarians, pharmacists, chiropractors, accountants, and other professionals.

In order to have a goodwill value, the spouse must have an ownership interest in the business. If they are an employee only, there will be no goodwill value. If you believe your spouse may have a goodwill value due to a professional ownership interest, discuss this with your attorney. Your attorney will hire a qualified accountant or business valuation expert to determine any goodwill value.

As with business valuations, there are usually only a few attorneys in each county who are highly experienced in goodwill valuations. If there is a professional practice at issue in your case, seek an attorney with substantial experience in this area.

11.29 My spouse and I own and operate an agricultural operation. What do I need to know about dividing our assets?

Agricultural operations can be complex because income and debts can be derived from many sources. Unfortunately, such operations also readily provide for the hiding of assets. Your attorney will need to conduct discovery to determine whether all assets have been declared. Look for an attorney experienced in agricultural divorces and familiar with all aspects of federal programs. These are some of the actions that may be necessary in your case:

- Sending copies of your temporary restraining order regarding property to financial institutions, sale barns, major customers, or agencies that might be involved with the transfer of the farm assets

- Conducting more-in-depth discovery in order to gather information such as the timing of payments, contracts, agreements to withhold payment, prepurchased feed or fertilizer, and grain delivered but not receipted, and the value and location of all assets held

- Obtaining information from federal agencies such as the Department of Agriculture or the Farm Credit Administration

- Using a forensic accountant to help investigate, including evaluating balance sheets and tracing cash flow

- Hiring an appraiser to value the land, equipment, livestock, and agricultural products

Work closely with your attorney to be sure you have a complete and accurate picture of your financial situation before entering into settlement negotiations or proceeding to trial.

11.30 My spouse says I'm not entitled to a share of his stock options because he gets to keep it only if he stays employed with his company. What are my rights?

Stock options are often a very valuable asset. They are also one of the most complex issues when dividing assets during a divorce. Some challenges include:

- Each company has its own rules about awarding and exercising stock options.

- Complete information is needed from the employer.

- There are different methods for calculating the value of stock options.

- The reasons the options were given can impact the valuation and division.

- There are cost and tax considerations when options are exercised.

If either you or your spouse owns stock options, begin discussing this asset with your attorney early in the case to allow sufficient time to settle the issues or to be well prepared for trial. If there are stock options, you are likely entitled to a share of their value. Always ensure the options are properly valued. Usually, a qualified CPA is hired to assist in this process.

11.31 What is a *prenuptial agreement* and how might it affect the property settlement phase of the divorce?

A *prenuptial agreement* is a contract entered into between two people prior to their marriage. It can include provisions for how assets and debts will be divided in the event the marriage is terminated, as well as provisions regarding spousal maintenance and attorney fees. Your property settlement is likely to be impacted by the terms of your prenuptial agreement if the agreement is upheld as valid by the court.

Because prenuptial agreements can have a very substantial impact upon the marital estate, courts look at prenuptial agreements very closely. If the prenuptial agreement fails to meet certain legal standards, it can be invalidated by a court, either in whole or in part. The court may consider many factors in determining whether to uphold your prenuptial agreement. Among the factors are:

- Whether your agreement was entered into voluntarily. This includes whether the agreement was signed far enough in advance of the wedding so undue pressure was not placed upon the spouse. Agreements signed close to the wedding date risk being invalidated

- Whether your agreement was fair and reasonable at the time it was signed

- Whether you and your spouse gave a complete disclosure of your assets and debts

- Whether you and your spouse each had your own attorney

- Whether you and your spouse each had enough time to consider the agreement

If you have a prenuptial agreement, bring a copy of it to the initial consultation with your attorney. Be sure to provide your attorney with a detailed history of the facts and circumstances surrounding reaching and signing the agreement. Listen to your attorney's advice as to whether to challenge the prenuptial agreement and attempt to invalidate it.

11.32 Will debts be considered when determining the division of the property?

Yes. The court will consider any debts incurred during the course of the marriage when dividing the property. For example, if you are awarded a car valued at $12,000, but you owe a $10,000 debt on the same vehicle, the court will take that debt into consideration in the overall division of the assets. Similarly, if one spouse agrees to pay substantial marital credit card debt, this obligation will be considered in the final determination of the division of property and debts.

If your spouse incurred debts that you believe should be his or her sole responsibility, tell your attorney. Some debts incurred during the marriage may still be treated separately by the court from other debts incurred during the marriage. For example, if your spouse spent large sums of money on gambling, affairs, or other frivolous pursuits with no marital value, you may be able to argue that those debts should be the sole responsibility of your spouse.

Generally, debts incurred before the marriage or after separation are the separate debt of the spouse incurring them. It is usually not considered as part of the marital estate. They may be relevant, however, as to a need for spousal maintenance.

11.33 What is a *property settlement agreement*?

A *property settlement agreement* is a written document that includes all of the financial agreements you and your spouse have reached in your divorce. This may include the division of property and debts. If the parties have a broader agreement, spousal maintenance, child support, and attorney fees may also be included into the agreement. Once this agreement is signed by the spouses and their respective attorneys, it is enforceable by the court as a contract even if one party should decide to try to back out of the agreement. For this reason, a spouse should be sure it is the agreement he or she wants to be bound to before signing it.

The property settlement may be filed with the court as a separate document. By doing so, parties can finalize their property matters even before they are eligible to become divorced. The agreement reached in the settlement agreement is usually incorporated by reference into the decree of dissolution when it is entered with the court at a later date.

11.34 What happens after my spouse and I approve the property settlement agreement? Do we still have to go to court?

Not necessarily. After you and your spouse approve and sign the property settlement agreement, a decree of dissolution and supporting documents must still be drafted and presented to the judge for approval and signature. If there are some disputes over the terms of the decree or supporting documents, a court hearing may still be required to resolve these disputes. If all parties remain in agreement, however, a formal court hearing is not required and the dissolution documents can be presented to the judge for signature by your attorney without you having to appear in court.

11.35 If my spouse and I think our property settlement agreement is fair, why does the judge have to approve it?

The judge has a duty to ensure all property settlement agreements in divorces are fair, reasonable, and equitable under Washington law. For this reason, your judge must review your agreement especially with regard to child-support provisions, parenting plan issues, and jurisdiction issues. The judge can consider the facts and circumstances of your case when reviewing the agreement. Unless something is unusual, the judge will usually approve the agreements reached by the parties and their attorneys.

11.36 What happens to the property distribution if one of us dies before the divorce proceedings are completed?

If your spouse dies prior to your divorce decree being entered, you will be considered married and treated as a surviving spouse under the law. The divorce process is terminated. The matter then becomes one of division of the decedent's estate.

11.37 After our divorce is final, can the property award be modified?

Generally, provisions in your property settlement agreement or decree dealing with the distribution of your assets and debts are not modifiable. Absent an uncommon instance of fraud, duress, or newly discovered evidence, the property settlement agreement cannot be modified. However, community property that was not divided in the decree remains jointly owned by the parties. If such property later discovered, the court will divide it after the decree.

12

Benefits: Insurance, Retirement, and Pensions

During your marriage, you might have taken certain employment benefits for granted. You might not have given much thought each month to having insurance through your spouse's work. Your retirement planning never considered the loss of benefits due to a divorce. Suddenly, these benefits come to the forefront of your mind once a divorce is filed. You quickly realize you need a better understanding of how the courts will divide these employment-related benefits.

12.1 Will my children continue to have health coverage through my spouse's work even though we're divorcing?

If either you or your spouse currently provides health insurance for your children, it is very likely the court will order the insurance to remain in place until your child reaches the age of majority, or for so long as it remains available, and support is being paid for your child. There are limits, however, on how much the court can order a parent to pay for health insurance; this limit is essentially derived from the spouse's income. The cost of insurance for the children will be taken into consideration in determining the amount of child support to be paid.

12.2 Will I continue to have health insurance through my spouse's work after the divorce?

It depends. Initially, you should remain covered during the pendency of the divorce. However, most insurance companies refuse to treat a person as a spouse after the entry of the divorce decree.

Investigate the cost of continuing on your spouse's employer-provided plans under a federal law known as *COBRA* after the expiration of your previous coverage. This coverage can be maintained for up to three years. However, the cost can be very high, so you will want to determine whether it is a realistic option. Begin early in investigating your eligibility for coverage on your spouse's health insurance plan after the entry of the decree, and your options for your future health insurance. The cost of your health care is an important factor when pursuing spousal support and planning your postdivorce budget.

12.3 Is there a way to finalize my separation and keep medical insurance?

If medical insurance is a substantial concern, talk with your attorney about finalizing the matter as a legal separation. A legal separation provides for a final property and debt division, provides for a final child-support order, and provides for a final parenting plan. However, the parties remain married after the decree of legal separation is entered. By remaining married, a spouse is generally still eligible for continuing medical coverage. However, this would require the cooperation of both spouses. It may be a good option to consider for someone who is otherwise uninsurable or who would incur very high continuing coverage.

12.4 When does the qualified domestic relations order get entered?

As mentioned earlier, a qualified domestic relations order (QDRO) is a court order that requires a retirement or pension plan administrator pay you the share of your former spouse's retirement that was awarded to you in the decree. These orders help ensure a nonemployee spouse receives his or her share directly from the employee spouse's plan.

Obtaining a QDRO is a critical step in the divorce process. They can be complex documents, and a number of steps are required to reduce future concerns about enforcement and to fully protect your rights. These court orders must comply with numerous technical rules and be approved by the plan administrator, which is often located outside Washington. Whenever possible, court orders dividing retirement plans should be entered at the same time as the decree of dissolution, or very soon thereafter, in order to avoid transfer of accounts or loss of value due to market fluctuations or risky investment practices.

12.5 How many years must I have been married before I'm eligible to receive a part of my spouse's retirement fund or pension?

Generally, any portion of a retirement that is earned during the marriage may be considered by the court for valuation and an equitable distribution. No minimum number of years of marriage must be met for a spouse to receive a share of the other's retirement interests. For example, if you were married for three years and your spouse contributed $10,000 to a 401(k) plan during the marriage, it is likely the court would award you half of the value of the contribution when dividing your property and debts. There are some exceptions to this rule, but such exceptions are rare and usually involve pensions controlled by federal law, such as railroad retirements, military disability retirements, or Social Security. Even then, a court can provide a valuation offset from other marital assets.

While the length of the marriage may not impact your ability to be compensated for the value of the retirement interests earned during marriage, it may impact your ability to receive your share of the retirement directly from the employer. For example, a marriage must be of sufficient duration to receive military retirement payment directly from the government. In such cases, a spouse could be ordered to send the other spouse a share of the payment after it is received each month. This has fairly obvious problems where the spouse receiving the retirement is not motivated to assist the other spouse. Usually, it is a better idea under these circumstances to simply offset your value of the retirement against other marital assets that are easily divisible. Talk with your attorney about your options when it comes to the division of any retirement interest.

12.6   I contributed to my pension plan for ten years before I got married. Will my spouse get half of my entire pension?

Probably not. It is more likely the court will award your spouse only a portion of your retirement that was acquired during the marriage. If you or your spouse made premarital contributions to a pension or retirement plan, be sure to let your attorney know. This information is essential to determine which portion of the retirement plan should be treated as separate property and thus unlikely to be shared.

12.7   I plan to keep my same job after my divorce. Will my former spouse get half of the money I contribute to my retirement plan after my divorce?

No. Your former spouse should be entitled to only the portion of your retirement accumulated during the marriage. Talk with your attorney so that the language of the court order ensures protection of your postdivorce retirement contributions. Careless drafting of the divorce decree has been known to inadvertently cause a spouse to lose retirement interests earned after the divorce.

12.8   Am I still entitled to a share of my spouse's retirement plan even though I never contributed to one of my own plans during our marriage?

Yes. Retirement plans are often the most valuable asset accumulated during a marriage. Consequently, your judge will consider the retirement plans along with all of the other marital assets and debts when determining a fair division. If the judge does not award you a portion of a retirement plan, it is only because the judge will award you other property of similar value.

12.9   How will I know the exact amount of my future monthly pension payment after the divorce?

More than one factor will determine your rights in collecting from your spouse's retirement plan. One factor will be the terms of the court order dividing the retirement. The court order will tell you whether you are entitled to a set dollar amount, a percentage, or a fraction to be determined based upon the length of your marriage and how long your spouse continues working. For a defined benefit plan, such as a pension, the fraction used by the court to determine how much you are eligible to receive will be the number of years you were married while your spouse was employed at that company divided by the total number of years your spouse is employed with the company.

Another factor will be the terms of the retirement plan itself. Some provide for lump-sum withdrawals while others issue payments in monthly installments. Review the terms of your court order with your attorney and contact the plan administrator to obtain the clearest understanding of your rights and benefits. While the exact amount of the pension payment may be unknown, you should be able to arrive at a fairly accurate estimation of the monthly benefit for retirement planning purposes.

12.10 If I am eligible to receive my spouse's retirement benefits, when am I eligible to begin collecting it? Do I have to be sixty-five to collect it?

It depends upon the terms of your spouse's retirement plan. Usually you will begin to receive benefits when your spouse begins to receive them. However, in some cases it is possible to begin receiving your share at the earliest date your spouse is eligible to receive them, regardless of whether he or she elects to do so. Military retirements are shared when benefits commence, often long before the age of sixty-five. Union-related retirement benefits often begin before age sixty-five. Police and firefighter benefits may begin before age sixty-five. There are many other examples. Check the terms of your spouse's plan with your attorney or with the plan administrator to learn your options. Plan administrators are usually very cooperative, especially those affiliated with government retirement plans. A substantial amount of information is also available on the Internet.

12.11 Am I entitled to cost-of-living increases on my share of my spouse's retirement?

It depends. If your spouse has a retirement plan that includes a provision for a *cost-of-living allowance (COLA)*, talk to your attorney about whether this can be included in the court order dividing the retirement. If you fail to include language in the court order about the receipt of COLA benefits, you substantially risk losing them.

12.12 What circumstances might prevent me from receiving a portion of my spouse's retirement benefits?

Some government pension plans, if they are in lieu of Social Security benefits or are disability related, are not subject to division but can be potentially offset against other assets. Retirement benefits earned before marriage or after separation are not usually shared. Sometimes, a court might choose to award a spouse an asset of equal value rather than go through the hassles and expenses of dividing a retirement interest.

12.13 Does the death of my spouse affect the payout of retirement benefits to me or to our children?

It depends upon both the nature of your spouse's retirement plan and the terms of the court order dividing the retirement. The death of the spouse receiving benefits can cause the benefits to terminate. If you want to be eligible for survivorship benefits from your spouse's pension, discuss the issue with your attorney before your case is settled or goes to trial. If you fail to include a provision for survivor benefits in your court order, you risk permanently losing these benefits. Keep in mind that a survivor benefit option, where it exists, is not free. It may not be worth electing due to the cost involved as opposed to the risk of death. Carefully discuss the risks and benefits of a survivor benefit option with your attorney.

12.14 Can I still collect on my former spouse's Social Security benefits if he or she passes on before I do?

It depends. You may be eligible to receive benefits if:

- You were married to your spouse for ten or more years.
- You are not remarried.
- You are at least sixty-two years old.
- The benefit you would receive based on your own earning record is less than the benefit you would receive from your former spouse.

169

For more information, contact your local Social Security Administration office or visit the SSA website at www.ssa.gov.

12.15 What orders might the court enter regarding life insurance?

The judge may order you or your spouse to maintain a life insurance policy to ensure future support payments are made, such as child support and spousal maintenance. However, in most cases you will be required to pay for your own life insurance after the divorce, and you should include this as an expense in your monthly budget. Also, discuss with your attorney when you can change your beneficiary. There may be some court-ordered restraints that limit your ability to change the beneficiary and permission from the court may be required.

12.16 What happens to the cash value of our life insurance policies?

Life insurance policies may have a cash value. Insurance policies that have a cash value are typically known as *whole life insurance policies.* Whole life policy premiums are typically more expensive than term life policies because they build a growing cash value as the policy payments are made. Even if payments stop, these whole life policies can be "cashed in," and a spouse would receive the current cash value that exists at the time the policy is cashed in.

Term life insurance policies typically have no value other than the death benefit itself. Once payments stop, the policy ends and there is no value. Because they do not have a cash value, the cost of term life insurance is typically cheaper than whole life insurance. The majority of life insurance policies are term life policies.

The court may award the whole life insurance policy to a spouse. This spouse will then be charged with the value of the whole life policy in the overall distribution of property. Where resources are minimal and debts are high, the court may order that the whole life policy be cashed in and the funds used to meet immediate financial obligations, or shared between the spouses.

12.17 My spouse is in the military. What are my rights to benefits after the divorce?

As the former spouse of a military member, the types of benefits to which you may be entitled are typically determined by the number of years you were married, the number of years your spouse was in the military while you were married, and whether or not you have remarried. Be sure you obtain accurate information about these dates.

Among the benefits for which you may be eligible are:

- A portion of your spouse's military retirement pay
- A survivor benefit in the event of your spouse's death
- Health care or participation in a temporary, transitional health care program
- Ability to keep your military identification card
- Use of certain military facilities, such as the commissary

While your divorce is pending, educate yourself about your right to future military benefits so you can plan for your future with clarity. Contact your base legal office, or for more information, visit the website for the branch of the military of which your spouse was a member. The military is helpful in explaining benefits to a spouse, but you should still consult with your own attorney on these issues.

13

Division of Debts

Throughout a marriage, most couples will have disagreements about money from time to time. You might think extra money should be spent on a family vacation, while your spouse may insist that it should be saved for your retirement. You may think it is time to finally buy a new car, but your spouse thinks driving the ten-year-old minivan for two more years is a better idea. If you and your spouse had different philosophies about saving and spending during your marriage, chances are that you will have some differing opinions when dividing your debts in divorce.

Washington law provides that the payment of debts must also be taken into consideration when dividing the assets from your marriage. There are steps you can take to ensure the best outcome possible when it comes to dividing your marital debt. These include providing accurate and complete debt information to your attorney and asking your attorney to include provisions in your divorce decree to protect you in the future if your spouse refuses to pay his or her share. You should take steps to avoid being damaged if your spouse files for bankruptcy. It is important to create a divorce decree that will lead to financial security as you seek a fresh start after your divorce is final.

13.1 Who is responsible for paying credit card bills and making house payments during the divorce proceedings?

In most cases, the court will make decisions regarding the payment of credit card debt, lines of credit, vehicle loans, mortgages, and other debts on a temporary basis. In order for this to occur, you must file a motion for temporary orders with the court and set up a hearing date. The court will analyze the financial resources and income of the parties, and then order each spouse to pay an equitable share of the debts based on available financial resources. The spouse with more available income generally will pay more of the debts.

Often, the spouse who remains in the home will be responsible for mortgage payments, taxes, utilities, and other ordinary expenses. The same rationale applies to vehicle loans or student loans. The spouse with the vehicle or the resulting education is generally ordered to pay these debts. This is not a hard-and-fast rule though. The spouse with the home or the vehicle may not have the financial ability to make these payments, which is common in the cases of stay-at-home parents or parents who worked part-time while caring for the children. In these cases, the court may order the other spouse to make these debt payments or to pay spousal maintenance so their spouse can meet these obligations.

Sometimes, the amount of debt exceeds the ability of the spouses to pay these debts. It is not uncommon that spouses had a hard time paying all of their debts while they were together in one household. In these cases, it will likely be impossible to pay the debts when two households must now be supported on the same amount of income. In these cases, the court may order that only the most important debts be paid (such as the house, vehicle, or insurance) or that assets be sold in order to pay the debts.

If you are concerned you cannot afford to stay in the marital home on a temporary basis, talk with your attorney about your options prior to the temporary hearing. Once child support and spousal maintenance payments are factored in, you may be able to afford the costs of the staying in the marital home. If funds are particularly grim, it may be time to consider selling the family home and finding more-affordable housing.

Of course, the parties can always agree to an equitable division of the debts without the need for a court hearing. Work with your attorney and spouse to reach a temporary agreement, which can be entered with the court as a temporary order. Discuss the importance of making at least minimum payments on time to avoid substantial finance charges, late fees, and damage to your credit.

13.2   What, if anything, should I be doing with the credit card companies as we go through the divorce?

Begin by obtaining a copy of your credit report from at least two of the three nationwide consumer reporting companies: Experian, Equifax, and TransUnion. *The Fair Credit Reporting Act* entitles you to a free copy of your credit report from each of these three companies every twelve months. Your spouse may have incurred debt using your name. This information is important to relay to your attorney and you can determine if this is an issue from reviewing your credit report.

If the other spouse was ordered to pay credit cards or other debts in your name, monitor these debts monthly to ensure that the payments are timely. Your credit will be damaged if your spouse does not make timely payments on accounts on which your name appears. It does not matter if a court ordered the other spouse to make the payment when it comes to protecting your credit. If you find payments are late or have not been made, contact your attorney immediately so these issues can be addressed before damage to your credit is too great.

If you and your spouse have joint credit card accounts, it is advisable to begin the process of removing a spouse as an authorized user or to close the account. Be sure to consult with your attorney to determine if temporary restraining orders, often entered in a case, prohibit you from making changes to credit cards. Unless your attorney advises otherwise, it is generally best to be open with the other spouse about which credit cards are being closed or having the other spouse removed as an authorized user.

13.3 How is credit card debt divided in the final divorce decree?

Credit card debt will be divided as a part of the overall division of the marital property and debts. Just as in the division of property, the court considers what is equitable or fair, in your case. The judge will try to divide the debt in a way that makes the most sense. A mortgage loan will be usually awarded to the spouse receiving the house. The vehicle loan will go to the spouse receiving the vehicle. A 401(k) loan goes to the spouse with the 401(k). Credit card debts usually go to the spouse whose name appears on the credit card as they have the greatest incentive to make the payment. Student loans go to the spouse who received the education.

The judge is concerned with the net equity, rather than the total value of the estate or the total value of the debts. If the marital estate is worth $300,000 and there is $100,000 in mortgage, car loan, and credit card debt, the net estate is $200,000. The judge wants to then ensure that each party receives something close to $100,000 of net equity each (50 percent of the net estate to each spouse).

Keep in mind though, that Washington is an equitable distribution state. The judge is not required to grant each party 50 percent of the net estate. If there are significant differences in the incomes of the parties or other equitable factors present, the judge may award 55 percent, 60 percent, 70 percent, or even more of the net estate to the financially disadvantaged spouse. Ask your attorney if you may be entitled to receive more than 50 percent of the net estate.

13.4 Am I responsible for repayment of my spouse's student loans?

It depends. This is certainly a grey area and different courts may have different opinions. If your spouse incurred student loans prior to the marriage, it is most likely that he or she will be ordered to pay that debt.

If the debt was incurred during the marriage, how the funds were used may have an impact on who is ordered to pay them. For example, if your spouse borrowed $10,000 during the marriage for tuition, it is likely your spouse will be ordered to pay that debt. However, if a $10,000 student loan was taken out by your spouse, but $5,000 of it was used for a family vacation, to pay other debt, to buy furniture, or for other family purposes, then the court is more likely to order the debt shared.

13.5   During the divorce proceedings, am I still responsible for debt my spouse continues to accrue?

Probably not. In most cases, the court will order each of the parties to be responsible for his or her own post-separation debts. In some cases, the date for dividing debt is when the parties separated, and in others it is the date the petition for divorce was filed.

Even if the court were to order your spouse to pay debts incurred after separation, you may still have some problems with creditors. If your name is on the credit card or line of credit, the creditor may still decide to pursue you for the post-separation charges if your spouse defaults on payment. Even if you prevail against the creditors, your credit will likely be damaged and you will incur substantial costs in defending against the claims. This is why it is always better to have your name removed from the other spouse's credit card, to remove your spouse as an authorized user on your card, or to close the credit card entirely.

13.6   During the marriage my spouse applied for and received several credit cards without my knowledge. Am I responsible for them?

It depends. If the spouse used the credit cards for legitimate purposes, such as food, clothes, furnishings, household goods, etc., the debt will probably be considered a community debt and factored into the overall equitable distribution of the marital estate. If the cards were used for purposes such as gambling, gifts to others, pornography, or other uses with no benefit to the marital community, the court is not likely to order it to be part of the equitable distribution marital estate. The credit card companies are unlikely to pursue you in collection since your name does not appear on the account.

13.7 During our marriage, we paid off thousands of dollars of debt incurred by my spouse before we were married. Will the court take this into consideration when dividing our property and debt?

It may. Just as premarital assets can have an impact on the overall division of property and debts, so can premarital debt. Depending upon the length of the marriage, the evidence of the debt, and the amount paid, it may be a factor for the judge to consider when making an equitable distribution of the marital estate. Be sure to let your attorney know if either you or your spouse brought substantial debt into the marriage.

13.8 Regarding debts, what is a *hold-harmless clause*, and why should it be in the divorce decree?

A *hold-harmless* provision is intended to protect you in the event your spouse fails to follow a court order to pay a debt after the divorce is granted. The language typically provides your spouse shall "indemnify and hold [you] harmless from liability" on the debt. If you and your spouse have a joint debt and your spouse fails to pay, the creditor may nevertheless attempt to collect from you. This is because the court is without power to change the creditor's rights and can make orders affecting only you and your spouse. In the event your spouse fails to pay a court-ordered debt and the creditor attempts collection from you, the hold-harmless provision in your divorce decree can be used in an effort to recover payment and attorney fees from your former spouse.

13.9 Why do my former spouse's doctors say they have a legal right to collect from me for bills incurred during my marriage when my former spouse was ordered to pay her own medical bills?

Under Washington law, a debt incurred during marriage is a community debt. Your divorce decree does not take away the legal rights of creditors to collect community debts. The creditor can collect from either spouse, regardless of what the divorce decree orders. This potential problem requires you to insist on hold-harmless language in the divorce decree. Further, if you believe your spouse is likely to default on payments, you should consider taking the debt and receiving a greater share of marital assets to compensate you for taking this debt.

13.10 My spouse and I have agreed I will keep our home. Why must I refinance the mortgage?

There may be a number of reasons why your spouse is asking you to refinance the mortgage. First, the mortgage company cannot be forced to take your spouse's name off of the mortgage note. This means if you did not make the house payments, the lender could pursue collection against your spouse. Additionally, the spouse's credit will be damaged. This mortgage debt may also prevent him or her from getting a future mortgage to buy a new home.

Second, your spouse may want to receive his or her share of the home equity. It may be possible for you to borrow additional money at the time of refinancing to pay your spouse his or her share of the equity in the home. Sometimes, home equity is the only asset available for distribution.

While it is desirable for a home to be refinanced in order to remove the other spouse's name, this may not be required by the court. This is particularly true if the spouse would not qualify for a refinance or if the new interest rate would be substantially higher than the existing interest rate.

13.11 Can I file for bankruptcy while my divorce is pending?

Yes. Consult with your attorney if you are considering filing for bankruptcy while your divorce is pending. It will be important for you to ask questions such as:

- Should I file for bankruptcy on my own or with my spouse?
- How will filing for bankruptcy affect my ability to purchase a home in the future?
- Which debts can be discharged in bankruptcy and which cannot?
- How will a bankruptcy affect the division of property and debts in the divorce?

- How might a delay in the divorce proceeding due to a bankruptcy impact my case?
- What form of bankruptcy is best for my situation?

If you use a different attorney for your bankruptcy than for your divorce, be sure each attorney is kept fully informed about the developments in the other case.

13.12 What happens if my spouse files for bankruptcy during our divorce?

The filing of a bankruptcy while your divorce is pending can have a significant impact on your divorce. The bankruptcy may cause a delay. Additionally, you may now be required to pay all or some of the debts discharged by your spouse. If this is the case, you may want to seek spousal maintenance; neither child support nor spousal maintenance can be discharged by a bankruptcy. You may also need to consider filing for bankruptcy yourself. It will be important for you to discuss your options with your attorney.

13.13 Can I file for divorce while I am in bankruptcy?

Yes, but you must receive the bankruptcy court's permission to proceed with the divorce. The bankruptcy may cause a delay in some of your divorce proceedings. Also, the bankruptcy's "automatic stay" can prevent the divorce court from dividing property and liabilities between you and your spouse until you obtain the bankruptcy court's permission to proceed with the divorce. Generally, the bankruptcy action will not prevent either spouse from seeking child support or maintenance.

13.14 What should I do if my former spouse files for bankruptcy after our divorce and how can I protect myself from this in the divorce?

Contact your attorney immediately. If you learn your former spouse has filed for bankruptcy, you may have certain rights to object to the discharge of any debts your spouse was ordered to pay under your divorce decree. If you fail to take action, it is possible you will be held responsible for debts your spouse was ordered to pay.

It is generally better to try to protect yourself from bankruptcy during the divorce itself, rather than seek relief in bankruptcy court after the fact. If you feel your spouse may file for bankruptcy, you should try to structure the asset and debt division in your divorce decree in a way in which you will be best protected. Ask your attorney whether there are signs or risk of bankruptcy present in your case.

Assume your spouse receives $50,000 of property in the divorce and also receives $50,000 of debt. The spouse files for bankruptcy and discharges the $50,000 of debt. He has just received a "free" $50,000 because he still keeps the property. Worse, that $50,000 of debt may be passed to you, leaving you with far more debt than assets received in the divorce.

Where you suspect your spouse may file for bankruptcy, you should try to take the debt, if possible, and receive more of the property, thereby protecting yourself from potentially disastrous results. In taking on the debt, you should first take debts on which your name appears. The complexities of this situation require you to carefully consult with your attorney on these issues.

13.15 If I am awarded child support or spousal maintenance in my decree, can these obligations be discharged if my former spouse files for bankruptcy after our divorce?

No, support obligations such as child support and spousal maintenance are not dischargeable in bankruptcy, meaning these debts cannot be eliminated in a bankruptcy proceeding. Still, contact your attorney immediately if you learn that your former spouse has filed for bankruptcy. You may still need to file an objection in the bankruptcy court depending on what items your spouse seeks to discharge.

14

Taxes

Nobody likes a surprise letter from the Internal Revenue Service saying he or she owes more taxes. When your divorce is over, you want to be sure you don't later discover you owe taxes you weren't expecting to pay. A number of tax issues may arise during your divorce. Your attorney may not be able to answer all of your tax questions, so you may need to consult with an accountant or tax advisor for additional advice.

Taxes are important considerations in both settlement negotiations and trial preparation. They should not be overlooked. Taxes can impact many of your decisions, including those regarding spousal maintenance, division of property, and the receipt of benefits.

14.1 Will either my spouse or I have to pay income tax when we transfer property or pay a property settlement to one another according to our divorce decree?

No. However, it is important that you see the future tax consequences of a subsequent withdrawal, sale, or transfer of certain assets you receive in your divorce. Ask your attorney to take tax consequences into consideration when looking at the division of your assets.

14.2 Is the amount of child support I pay tax deductible?

No. Only payments that the court has characterized as maintenance are tax deductible. If tax deductibility is important to you, talk with your attorney about the possibility of re-characterizing some child support as spousal maintenance.

14.3   Do I have to pay income tax on any child support I receive?

No. Your child support is tax free regardless of when it is paid or when it is received.

14.4   What does the IRS consider spousal maintenance?

Not all payments made pursuant to a divorce or separation decree are deemed spousal maintenance. Maintenance does not include child support, property settlements and distributions, payments made to maintain property, or attorney fees. Amounts paid under a temporary order, divorce decree, or pursuant to a written separation agreement entered into between you and your spouse will be considered spousal maintenance if:

- You and your spouse or former spouse do not file a joint return with each other.

- The payment is in cash (including checks or money orders).

- The payment is received by (or on behalf of) your spouse or former spouse.

- You and your former spouse are not members of the same household when you make the payment.

- You have no liability to make the payment (in cash or property) after the death of your spouse or former spouse.

- Your payment is not treated as child support or a property settlement.

14.5   Is the amount of maintenance I am ordered to pay tax deductible?

Yes. Maintenance paid pursuant to a court order is tax deductible. Your tax deduction is a factor to consider when determining an appropriate amount of maintenance to be paid in your case.

14.6   Do I have to pay tax on the maintenance that I receive?

Yes. You must pay income tax on spousal maintenance you receive. Income tax is a critical factor in determining an appropriate amount of maintenance. If your "need" is for $2,000 in maintenance, and the court awards $2,000 in maintenance, you have a problem. Once the tax is paid, you will actually receive less than $2,000 and not be able to meet your monthly need. As a result, you must request increased maintenance to account for taxes so that your need is actually met. Be sure to consult with your tax advisor about payment of tax on your spousal maintenance.

14.7 During the divorce proceedings, is our tax filing status affected?

It can be. You are considered single if your decree is final by December 31 of the tax year. Under Washington law, your decree becomes final the day the judge signs it. If you are considered unmarried, your filing status is either "single" or, under certain circumstances, "head of household." If your decree is not final as of December 31, you remain married for tax purposes.

Talk to both your tax advisor and attorney about your filing status. It may be beneficial to figure out your tax on both a joint return and a separate return to see which gives you the lower tax. If practical, you can delay the entry of your divorce into the next calendar year in order to maximize tax benefits.

14.8 Should I file a joint income tax return with my spouse while our divorce is pending?

Consult your tax advisor to determine the risks and benefits of filing a joint return with your spouse. Compare this with the consequences of filing your tax return separately. Often, the overall tax liability will be less with the filing of a joint return, but other factors are important to consider.

When deciding whether to file a joint return with your spouse, consider any concerns you have about the accuracy and truthfulness of the information on the tax return. If you have any doubts, consult both your attorney and tax advisor before agreeing to sign a joint tax return with your spouse. You will want to avoid filing jointly with your spouse if you believe your spouse's "numbers" are fraudulent in any way. Prior to filing a return with your spouse, try to reach agreement about how any tax owed or refund expected will be shared, and ask your attorney to assist you in getting this in writing.

14.9 My spouse will not cooperate in providing the necessary documents to prepare or file our taxes jointly. What options do I have?

Talk with your attorney about requiring your spouse to cooperate in producing the necessary documents. Your attorney can serve your spouse with discovery requiring the production of these documents. If the spouse still refuses to provide the required documents, the court will compel him or her to do so. Although a judge cannot order your spouse to sign a joint return, the judge can order financial adjustments against him or her. These adjustments generally compensate a spouse for the increased tax incurred due to the other spouse's unreasonable refusal to file a joint return.

14.10 What tax consequences should I consider regarding the sale of our real estate?

When real estate is sold, whether during your divorce or after, the sale may be subject to a capital gains tax. If your home was your primary residence and you meet certain requirements, you may be eligible to exclude any gain on the sale of the home. There may also be issues resulting from depreciation claimed on rental properties. Talk with your attorney and tax advisor early in the divorce process about your exposure to future taxes related to your real estate.

14.11 How might capital gains tax be a problem for me in the years after the divorce?

Future capital gains tax on the sale of property should be discussed with your attorney during the negotiation and trial preparation stages of your case. This is especially important if the sale of the property is imminent. Failure to do so may result in an unfair outcome.

As an example, suppose you agree your spouse will be awarded proceeds from the sale of your home valued at $200,000 after the real estate commission, and you will take the stock portfolio also valued at $200,000. Suppose, after the divorce, you decide to sell the stock. It is still valued at $200,000, but you learn that its original price was $120,000 and you must pay capital gains tax of 15 percent on the $80,000 of gain. You pay tax of $12,000, leaving you with a total of $188,000.

Meanwhile, your former spouse sells the marital home but pays no capital gains tax because he qualifies for the capital gains exemption. He is left with the full $200,000. Tax implications of your property division should always be discussed with your attorney, with support from your tax advisor as needed. Tax consequences can also result from the sale of rental homes and properties, depreciated property, or other assets.

14.12 During and after the divorce, who gets to claim the children as dependents?

The judge has discretion to determine which parent will be entitled to claim the children as exemptions for income tax purposes. Many judges order exemptions be shared or alternated where child support has been ordered. However, most judges will order the payor of child support be current on his or her child support obligation in order to be eligible to claim the income tax dependency exemption. Additionally, if one party has income so low or so high where he or she will not benefit from the dependency exemption, the court may award the exemption to the other parent.

14.13 My decree says I have to sign IRS Form 8332 so my former spouse can claim our child as an exemption, since I have custody. Should I sign it once for all future years?

No. Child custody and child support can be modified in the future. If there is a future modification of custody or support, which parent is entitled to claim your child as an exemption could change. The best practice is to provide your former spouse a timely copy of Form 8332 signed by you for the appropriate tax year only.

14.14 Can my spouse and I split the child-care tax credit?

No. Only the custodial parent is allowed to claim the credit. If you are a noncustodial parent and paying child care, talk to your attorney about how to address this issue in your divorce decree.

185

14.15 Do I have to pay taxes on the portion of my spouse's 401(k) that was awarded to me in the divorce?

If you have been awarded a portion of your former spouse's 401(k) or 403(b) retirement plan, any distribution of these funds to you will be subject to regular income tax. If you elect to receive all or a portion of these assets early (applicable if you are under age fifty-nine and one half), rather than keeping an account in your name or rolling over the assets to an IRA or other permitted retirement account, you will also incur early-withdrawal penalties in addition to incurring tax liabilities on this amount. Talk with your attorney and tax advisor to determine your best options.

14.16 Is the cost of getting a divorce, including my attorney fees, tax deductible under any circumstances?

Your legal fees for getting a divorce are generally not deductible. However, a portion of your attorney fees may be deductible if they are for:

- The collection of sums included in your gross income, such as spousal maintenance or interest income
- Advice regarding the determination of taxes or tax due
- The operation of your business rather than for the divorce itself

You may also be able to deduct fees you pay to appraisers or accountants who assist you in the divorce process. Talk to your tax advisor about whether any portion of your attorney fees or other expenses from your divorce is deductible.

14.17 Do I have to complete a new Form W-4 for my employer because of my divorce?

Completing a new Form W-4, Employee's Withholding Certificate, will help you to claim the proper withholding allowances based upon your marital status and exemptions. Also, if you receive maintenance, you may need to make arrangements for the tax due on the maintenance income. Consult with your tax advisor to ensure you are making the most preferable tax-planning decision.

14.18 What is *innocent spouse relief* and how can it help me?

Innocent spouse relief refers to a method of obtaining relief from the Internal Revenue Service for taxes you owe if your spouse or former spouse failed to report income, reported income improperly, or claimed improper deductions or credits on a joint income tax return filed during your marriage.

Numerous factors affect your eligibility for innocent spouse tax relief, such as:

- You would suffer a financial hardship if you were required to pay the tax.
- You did not significantly benefit from the unpaid taxes.
- Your suffered abuse during your marriage.
- You thought your spouse would pay the taxes on the original return.

Talk with your attorney or tax advisor if you are concerned about liability for taxes arising from joint tax returns filed during the marriage. You may benefit from a referral to an attorney who specializes in tax law.

15

Going to Court

For many of us, our images of going to court are created by movie scenes and our favorite television shows. We picture the witness breaking down in tears after a grueling cross-examination. We see attorneys waltzing around the courtroom, waving their arms as they plead the case to a jury. Hollywood drama, however, is a far cry from reality. Going to court for your divorce can mean many things, ranging from sitting in a hallway waiting for the attorneys and judge to conclude a conference, to being on the witness stand giving mundane answers to questions about your monthly living expenses.

Regardless of the nature of your court proceeding, going to court often evokes a sense of anxiety. Perhaps your divorce is the first time in your life you have been in a courtroom. Be assured that these feelings of nervousness and uncertainty are normal. In Washington, all divorce proceedings are held before a judicial officer. There are no juries. The judge understands the emotions you are going through and the stresses you are under.

Understanding what will occur in court and being well prepared for court hearings will relieve much of your stress. Knowing the order of events, courtroom etiquette, the role of the people in the courtroom, and what is expected of you will make the entire experience easier. Any time you go to court, your attorney will be with you for support. Remember, every court appearance moves you one step closer to completing your divorce so you can move forward with your life.

15.1 What do I need to know about appearing in court and court dates in general?

Court dates are important. As soon as you receive a notice from your attorney about a court date, confirm whether your attendance is required and mark the date on your calendar. Ask your attorney about the nature of the hearing, including whether the judge will be listening to testimony by witnesses, reading affidavits, or merely listening to the arguments of the attorneys.

Ask whether it is necessary for you to meet with your attorney or take any other action to prepare for the hearing, such as providing additional information or documents. Find out how long the hearing is expected to last. It may be as short as a few minutes or as long as a day or more.

If you plan to attend the hearing, determine where and when to meet your attorney. Depending upon the type of hearing, your attorney may want you to arrive in advance of the scheduled hearing time in order to further prepare. It is always best if you can attend your hearings, with the possible exception of minor scheduling hearings. By attending the hearings, you will have a better understanding of your case. You will also be able to ensure your attorney has properly presented your case. By hearing the judge's decision, you will also be able to understand what issues are important to your judge.

Tell your attorney you want to attend the hearings. If your attorney is reluctant to have you present for your hearing or does not notify you of a hearing, this may be a red flag. You may need to consider arranging for new counsel.

Make sure you know the location of the courthouse, where to park, and the floor and room number of the courtroom. Planning for such simple matters as having change for a parking meter can eliminate unnecessary stress. If you want someone to go to court with you to provide you support, first check with your attorney. However, Washington courts are usually open to all observers.

15.2 When and how often will I need to go to court?

When and how often you will need to go to court depends upon a number of factors. Depending upon the complexity of your case, you may have no hearings, have only one hearing, or numerous court hearings throughout the course of your divorce.

Some hearings, usually those on minor procedural matters, are attended only by the attorneys. These could include requests for the other side to provide information or for the setting of certain deadlines. These hearings are often brief. Other hearings, such as temporary hearings for custody or support, are lengthier and are typically attended by both parties and their attorneys.

If you and your spouse settle all of the issues in your case, your attendance at court will probably not be required. If your case proceeds to trial, your appearance will be required for the duration of the trial. In Washington, divorce matters are heard before a judge only. Juries do not hear divorce matters.

15.3   How much notice will I receive about appearing in court?

The amount of notice you will receive for any court hearing ranges from a few hours to several weeks. Emergency hearings are always possible in family law actions, particularly when children are the focus of the litigation. Emergency hearings typically provide very short notice. Standard family law hearings provide days or weeks of notice. If you receive a notice of a hearing, contact your attorney immediately to learn what steps are needed to prepare.

15.4   I am afraid to be alone in the same room with my spouse. When I go to court, is this going to happen if the attorneys go into the judge's chambers to discuss the case?

Talk to your attorney. Prior to any court hearing, you and your spouse may be asked to wait while your attorneys meet with the judge to discuss preliminary matters. A number of options are likely to be available to ensure you feel safe. These include having you or your spouse wait in different locations or having a friend or family member present. Usually a court clerk remains present in the court with you. Your attorney wants to support you in feeling secure throughout all court proceedings. Just let him or her know your concerns.

15.5 My spouse's attorney keeps asking for continuances of court dates. Is there anything I can do to stop this?

Continuances of court dates are not unusual in divorces. A continuance motion is a request that the court postpone the hearing to a new date in the future. Requests to postpone a hearing for one or two weeks are fairly common. A court date may be postponed for many reasons, including a conflict on the calendar of one of the attorneys or the judge, the lack of availability of one of the spouses or an important witness, or the need for more time to prepare. The court will often provide a party with a continuance if there is no "prejudice" shown to the other side. Prejudice means that something negative will occur if the hearing is postponed. However, courts frown on multiple continuance requests unless very good cause is shown. Discuss with your attorney your desire to move the case forward without further delay, so repeated requests for continuances can be opposed.

15.6 If I have to go to court, will I be put on the stand?

It depends on the type of proceeding. Most temporary orders hearings are done on declarations only. A *declaration* is a written statement that is signed by a witness under penalty of perjury. The judge reads these declarations before the hearing. At the hearing, only the attorneys speak and make an argument. The spouses do not testify and witnesses are not called to the stand. However, it is always possible the judge may ask the spouses some brief questions.

If a matter proceeds to trial, it is highly likely the spouses will testify. However, there are times when the only dispute is over valuations. In such cases, only the appraisers or accountants may be required to testify. Talk with you attorney about his or her strategy for your case.

15.7 My attorney said I need to be in court for our *temporary hearing* next week. What's going to happen?

A *temporary hearing* is held to determine such matters as who remains in the house while your divorce is pending, temporary custody, temporary support, and other financial matters. The procedure for the temporary hearing can vary depending upon the county in which your case was filed,

191

and the judge to which the case is assigned. Most temporary hearings are held on the basis of written affidavits and the arguments of the attorneys.

In some counties, your hearing will be one of numerous other hearings on the judge's calendar. You may find yourself in a courtroom with many other attorneys and clients, all having matters scheduled before the court that day. The spouses and the attorneys will be called up to the table in front of the judge when it is their turn for the hearing.

After the hearing is completed, immediately upon completion of argument by the attorneys, the judge will generally give a ruling on the issues. The attorneys are then expected to complete the orders to reflect the judge's decision. The judge will then sign the orders once they are prepared and presented.

In Washington, the temporary orders are often heard by *court commissioners*. Court commissioners are judicial officers who were appointed by Superior Court judges. This is more likely to be the case in larger counties. In smaller counties, the Superior Court judges may hear temporary order hearings. There may also be a blend of court commissioners and judges hearing the cases. Both Superior Court judges and court commissioners are judicial officers.

15.8 Do I have to go to court if all of the issues in my case are settled?

No. If you and your spouse settle all of the issues in your case, you are not required to testify in court. Your attorney can enter the final decree and related orders without your presence.

15.9 Are there any rules about courtroom etiquette that I need to know?

Knowing a few tips about being in the courtroom will make your experience easier.

- Dress appropriately. Avoid overly casual dress, a lot of jewelry, revealing clothing, and extreme hairstyles. For men, wear a nice pair of Levi's Dockers or similar-type pants and a polo or long-sleeved shirt. For females, a pant suit or a modest dress is appropriate. Avoid jeans, shorts, T-shirts, and tennis shoes.

192

- Do not bring beverages into the courtroom. Most courts have rules which do not allow food and drink in courtrooms. If you need water, ask your attorney.
- Dispose of chewing gum before entering the court.
- Do not talk aloud in the courtroom unless you are on the witness stand, being questioned by the judge, or taking with your attorney at appropriate times.
- Do not enter the judge's office or approach the bench (where the judge is seated) without the judge's permission.
- Stand up whenever the judge is entering or leaving the courtroom.
- Be sure to turn off your electronic devices and cell phones.
- Cover tattoos with clothing, if possible, and remove facial jewelry except for simple earrings for the female spouse. Many judges are quite conservative.
- Do not bring friends or family with you who present a poor image or who may be disruptive.
- Be mindful that the judge may be observing you during the hearing and a negative image may hurt your result.

15.10 What is the role of the *bailiff*?

The *bailiff,* also called a *judicial assistant,* provides support for the judge and attorneys in the management of the court calendar and the courtroom. The bailiff assists in the scheduling of court hearings and the management of legal documents given to the judge for review, such as temporary orders, briefs, and divorce decrees. Outside of the court hearings, parties are generally not allowed contact with the judge. All contact goes through the bailiff.

15.11 Will there be a *court reporter,* and what will he or she do?

A *court reporter* is a professional trained to make an accurate record of the words spoken and documents offered into evidence during court proceedings. Some counties use tape-recording devices rather than court reporters. A written transcript of a court proceeding may be purchased from the court reporter. If your case is appealed, the transcript prepared by the court reporter will be used by the appeals court to review the facts of your case.

Some hearings are held "off the record." This means that the court reporter is not making a record of what is being said. Ordinarily these are matters for which no appeal is expected to be taken and are generally procedural in nature.

15.12 Will I be able to talk to my attorney while we are in court?

During court proceedings it is important that your attorney give his or her full attention to anything being said by the judge, witnesses, or your spouse's attorney. For this reason, your attorney will avoid talking with you when anyone else in the courtroom is speaking. Plan to have pen and paper with you when you go to court. If your court proceeding is underway and your attorney is listening to what is being said by others in the courtroom, write a note with your questions or comments.

It is critical for your attorney to hear each question asked by the other attorney and all answers given by each witness. If not, opportunities for making objections to inappropriate evidence may be lost. You can support your attorney in doing an effective job for you by avoiding talking to him or her while a court hearing is in progress. If your court hearing is lengthy, breaks will be taken. You can use this time to discuss with your attorney any questions or observations you have about the proceeding.

15.13 What questions might my attorney ask me at the trial about the problems in our marriage and why I want the divorce?

Because Washington is a "no-fault" state, your attorney will ask you a brief question to show the court that the marriage is irretrievably broken, without going into detail about the specific difficulties in your marriage. The questioning will be similar to this:

Attorney: In your opinion, is your marriage irretrievably broken?
You: Yes.

It is unlikely you will be asked in great detail about the nature of the marital problems which led to the divorce unless it is relevant to other issues such as child custody. For example, an affair will not normally be discussed. However, if a child was exposed to sexual situations as a result of the affair, or assets were transferred to the new boyfriend or girlfriend, the affair may be discussed in more detail because of the relevance.

15.14 My attorney said the judge has issued a *case scheduling order* having to do with my divorce case and we will have to comply with it. What does this mean?

Ask your attorney for a copy of the *case scheduling order.* Some judges will order certain information be provided either to the opposing party or to the judge in advance of trial. The case scheduling order might include:

- The date by which all discovery must be completed
- The date by which witnesses must be disclosed
- The date by which exhibits must be disclosed
- The date by which mediation must be completed
- The date for your pretrial conference
- The date for your trial

15.15 What is a *pretrial conference*?

A *pretrial conference* is a meeting held with the attorneys and the judge to review information related to an upcoming trial, such as:

- How long the trial is expected to last
- The issues in dispute
- The law surrounding the disputed issues and when trial briefs will be provided
- The identification of witnesses
- The identification of trial exhibits
- The status of negotiations

If a pretrial conference is held in your case, ask your attorney whether you should attend. Often, the pretrial conference is merely a scheduling hearing attended only by the attorneys. Sometimes the pretrial conference may include a full hearing you should attend, often relating to a request by the other party to continue to trial.

15.16 Besides meeting with my attorney, is there anything else I should do to prepare for my upcoming trial?

Yes. Be sure to review your deposition and any information you provided in your discovery, such as answers to interrogatories. Also be sure to review any affidavits previously submitted to the judge, such as your financial declaration or child-support affidavit prepared for your temporary hearing. At trial, it is possible you will be asked some of the same questions. If you think you might give different answers at trial, discuss this with your attorney. It is important your attorney know in advance of trial whether any information you provided during the discovery process has changed.

15.17 I'm meeting with my attorney to prepare for trial. How do I make the most of these meetings?

Meeting with your attorney to prepare for your trial is important to achieving a good outcome. Come to the meeting prepared to discuss the following:

- The issues in your case
- Your desired outcome on each of the issues
- The questions you might be asked at trial by both attorneys
- The exhibits that will be offered into evidence during the trial
- The witnesses for your trial
- The status of negotiations

Meeting with your attorney will help you to better understand what to expect at trial and make the trial experience easier.

15.18 My attorney says the law firm is busy with *trial preparation*. What exactly is my attorney doing to prepare for my trial?

Countless tasks are necessary to prepare your case for trial. Trial is a very time=consuming process. Usually, a day of preparation is required for each day of trial. More preparation time is required when issues are especially complex, such as in significant-asset cases where a detailed financial tracing is required. These are some of the *trial preparations* tasks required:

- Developing arguments to be made on each of the contested issues
- Researching and reviewing the relevant law in your case
- Reviewing the facts of your case to determine which witnesses are best suited to testify about particular facts
- Reviewing, selecting, and preparing exhibits and compiling the exhibit books (a very time consuming process)
- Preparing questions for all witnesses
- Preparing an opening statement
- Reviewing rules on evidence to prepare for any objections to make or oppose at trial
- Determining the order of witnesses and all exhibits
- Drafting a trial brief for the judge
- Preparing your file for the day, including preparing a trial notebook with essential information

The attorney must be prepared in order to ensure a good outcome for you at trial. Proper preparation cannot be done in a matter of hours. Extensive trial preparation is a good sign that your attorney will make a very good presentation to the court.

15.19 How do I know who my witnesses will be at trial?

Well in advance of your trial date your attorney will discuss with you whether other witnesses, besides you and your spouse, will be necessary. Witnesses can include family members, friends, teachers, neighbors, child-care providers, counselors, clergy members, or others. When thinking of potential witnesses, consider your relationship with the witness, whether the witness has had an opportunity to observe relevant facts, and whether the witness has knowledge different from that of other witnesses.

You may also have expert witnesses testify on your behalf. An expert witness will provide opinion testimony based upon specialized knowledge, training, or experience. For example, a psychologist, real estate appraiser, or accountant may provide expert testimony on your behalf.

15.20 My divorce is scheduled for trial. Does this mean there is no hope for a settlement?

Many cases are settled after a trial date is set. The setting of a trial date may cause you and your spouse to think about the risks and costs of going to trial. This can help you both to focus on what is most important and lead you toward a negotiated settlement. Because the costs of preparing for and proceeding to trial are substantial, it is best to engage in settlement negotiations well in advance of your trial date. However, it is not uncommon for cases to settle a few days before trial or even at the courthouse soon before your trial begins.

15.21 Can I prevent my spouse from being in the courtroom?

Probably not. Because your spouse has a legal interest in the outcome of your divorce, he or she has a right to be present. Further, Washington courtrooms are open to the public. Consequently, it is not uncommon for persons not involved in your divorce to pass through the courtroom at various times simply because the person has other business with the court or because they want to watch the proceedings.

15.22 Can I take a friend or family member with me to court?

Yes. Let your attorney know in advance if you intend to bring anyone to court with you. Some people important to you may be emotional about your divorce or your spouse. Be sure to invite someone who is better able to focus attention on supporting you, rather than one who is emotional. Further, be aware if your friend is going to testify, he or she will probably not be allowed in the courtroom with you until their testimony is completed.

15.23 I want to do a great job testifying as a witness in my divorce trial. What are some tips?

Keep the following in mind to be a good witness on your own behalf:

- Listen carefully to the complete question before thinking of your answer. Wait to consider your answer until the full question is asked.

- Take your time. You may be asked questions that call for a thoughtful response. If you need a moment to reflect on an answer before you give it, allow yourself such time.

- Slow down. It is easy to speed up our speech when anxious. Taking your time with your answers ensures that the judge hears you and the court reporter can accurately record your testimony.

- If you don't understand a question or don't know the answer, be sure to say so.

- Tell the truth. Although this may not be always be comfortable, it is critical if you want the judge to believe your testimony.

- If the question calls for a "yes" or "no" answer, simply say so. Then wait for the attorney to ask you the next question. If there is more you want to explain, remember that you have already told your attorney all the important facts and he or she will make sure you are allowed to give any testimony significant to your case.

- Do not argue with the judge or the attorneys.

- Stop speaking if an objection is made by one of the attorneys. Wait until the judge has instructed you to answer.

- If you begin to feel emotional, your attorney can ask for a short break.

15.24 Should I be worried about being cross-examined by my spouse's attorney at trial?

If your case goes to trial, prepare to be asked some questions by your spouse's attorney. Many of these questions will call for a simple "yes" or "no." If you are worried about particular questions, discuss your concerns with your attorney. He or she can support you in giving a truthful response. Try not to take the questions personally, and never get angry in response to questions. Stay calm and professional as you give your answers. Remember you are simply doing your best to tell the truth about the facts.

15.25 What happens on the day of trial?

Although no two trials are alike, the following steps will occur in most divorce trials:

- Attorneys meet with the judge in chambers to discuss procedural issues, such as how many witnesses will be called, how long the case will take to present, and when breaks might be taken.
- Attorneys give opening statements.
- Petitioner's attorney calls petitioner's witnesses to testify. Respondent's attorney may cross-examine each of these witnesses.
- Respondent's attorney calls respondent's witness to testify. Petitioner's attorney may cross-examine each of these witnesses.
- Petitioner's attorney calls any rebuttal witnesses, that is, witnesses whose testimony contradicts the testimony of the respondent's witnesses.
- Closing arguments are made, first by the petitioner's attorney and then by the respondent's attorney.
- The judge gives his or her decision at some point following trial.

15.26 Will the judge decide my case the day I go to court?

Possibly. Often there is so much information for the judge to consider that it is not possible for him or her to give an immediate ruling. The judge may want to review documents, review the law, perform calculations, review his or her notes, and give thoughtful consideration to the issues to be decided. For this reason, it may be days or weeks before a ruling is made.

When a judge does not make a ruling immediately upon the conclusion of a trial, it is said the case has been "taken under advisement." The judge may call the attorneys and spouses back to court at a later date to give them the court's decision. At other times, the judge will complete a written decision and mail it to the attorneys.

16

The Appeals Process

You may find, despite your best efforts to settle your case that your divorce went to trial and the judge made major decisions seriously impacting your future. You may be disappointed by the judge's ruling. The judge might have seen your case differently than you and your attorney did. Perhaps the judge made mistakes. It may be that Washington law simply does not allow for the outcome you wanted.

Whatever the reasons for the court's rulings, you may feel that you cannot live with the judge's decisions. If this is the case, talk to your attorney immediately about your right to appeal. Together you can decide whether an appeal is in your best interests, or whether it is better to accept the court's ruling and invest your energy in moving forward with your future without an appeal.

16.1 How much time after my divorce do I have to file an appeal?

You must file an appeal within thirty days of the final order you wish to appeal. Because your attorney may also recommend filing certain motions following your trial, discuss your appeal rights with your attorney as soon as you have received the judge's ruling. A timely discussion with your attorney about your right to appeal is essential so important deadlines are not missed.

16.2 Can I appeal a temporary order?

Possibly. Under Washington law, only final orders may be appealed as a matter of right. Temporary orders may be appealed through a process known as a request for "discretionary review." The Court of Appeals only hears a request for discretionary review (appeals from temporary orders) if it feels it has significant merit which cannot wait for a final order. Most requests for discretionary review are denied.

16.3 What parts of the decree can be appealed?

If you or your spouse are unhappy with final decisions made by the judge in your case, either of you can file an appeal. Decisions that can be appealed include custody, parenting time, child support, maintenance, division of property, and attorney fees. In essence, virtually all aspects of a decision can be appealed. This does not necessarily mean it is wise to do so. The standard of review by the Court of Appeals varies with the type of issue being appealed, and some decisions are very difficult to successfully appeal. You will need to consult with your attorney as to which issues have a reasonable chance of success on appeal and which issues should be avoided.

16.4 When should an appeal be filed?

An appeal should only be filed when, after careful consultation with your attorney, you believe that the judge has made a serious error under the law or the facts of your case. Errors made in the application of law are much more likely to be reversed on appeal than errors that are based on facts (testimony and exhibits). Talk to your attorney at once if you are thinking about an appeal. Among the factors you should discuss with your attorney are:

- Whether the judge had the authority under the law to make the decisions set forth in your decree
- The likelihood of the success of your appeal
- The risk that an appeal by you will encourage an appeal by your former spouse
- The cost of the appeal
- The length of time an appeal can be expected to take
- The impact of a delay in the case during the appeal

The deadline for filing an appeal is thirty days from the date that a final order is entered in your case. It is important that you are clear about the deadline that applies in your case.

16.5   Are there any disadvantages to filing an appeal?

There can be disadvantages to filing an appeal, including:

- Increased attorney's fees and costs
- The risk of a worse outcome on appeal than you received at trial
- Delay
- Prolonged conflict between you and your former spouse
- Risk of a second trial occurring after the appeal
- Difficulty in obtaining closure and moving forward with your life

16.6   Is it necessary to have an attorney in order to appeal?

Technically, no. However, the appeals process is very detailed and specific, with set deadlines and specific court rules. Appellate briefs are required. Given the complex nature of the appellate process, you should have an attorney if you intend to file an appeal.

16.7   How long does the appeals process usually take?

It depends. An appeal can take anywhere from several months to over a year. An appeal may also result in the appellate court requiring further proceedings by the trial court. This will result in further delay. It is not unusual for an appeal to take over a year to be completed.

16.8   What are the steps in the appeals process?

There are many steps your attorney will take on your behalf in the appeal process, including:

- Identifying the issues to be appealed
- Filing a notice with the court of your intent to appeal
- Obtaining the necessary court documents and trial exhibits to send to the appellate court

- Obtaining a transcript of your trial, a written copy of testimony by witnesses and statements by the judge and the attorneys made in the presence of the court reporter. The transcript is very expensive and for a trial that lasted several days, it can cost thousands of dollars.

- Performing legal research to support your arguments on appeal

- Preparing and filing a document known as a *brief*, which sets forth the facts of the case and relevant law, complete with citations to court transcript, court documents, and prior cases

- Making an oral argument before the judges of the appellate court

- Reviewing the final decision received from the Court of Appeals

- Deciding whether to appeal to the Washington Supreme Court

16.9   Is filing and pursuing an appeal expensive?

Yes. In addition to filing fees and attorney fees, there is likely to be a substantial cost for the preparation of the transcript of the trial testimony.

16.10   If I do not file an appeal, can I ever go back to court to change my decree?

Certain aspects of a decree are not modifiable, such as the division of property and debts or the award of attorney fees. Other parts of your decree, such as child support, spousal maintenance, or matters regarding the children, may be modified provided there has been a "substantial change in circumstances." A modification of custody or parenting time for minor children will also require you to show that the change would be in their best interests.

If your decree did not provide for spousal maintenance, you will not be able to request it in the future. If you believe spousal maintenance should have been ordered, you may need to file an appeal. If you believe that a basis exists for a modification of your divorce decree, consult with your attorney.

17

What Happens after the Divorce?

You have finally reached the end of the divorce journey. You may be feeling sad about the end of your marriage but you may also be feeling hopeful about the future ahead of you. These feelings are normal.

It is also normal for you to feel uneasy about your attorney closing your file and that you will be without your divorce team to support you through the days ahead. You may be feeling overwhelmed and unsure about how to take the final actions to complete property transfers or name-change details. Whatever items are on your to-do list, it is best to map out your action plan. Understand which items are your responsibility and which items are the responsibility of your attorney.

17.1   What do I need to do when the amount of child support changes based on one of my children turning eighteen and graduating from high school?

This can actually be a very complex issue. The result depends on how your child-support order is drafted. If the support order provides for a single support transfer payment for all children, the child-support payment may not change when one child graduates from high school. If the support order breaks down the support transfer payment by child, then the obligor parent will pay the amount ordered for the remaining child(ren). In both situations, a modification of child support may be warranted. Ask your attorney if you should seek a modification under these circumstances. Failure to do so can result in very severe consequences and large judgments have been entered against parents who "assumed" that their support obligation automatically lowered with the graduation of a child.

17.2 Do I need to inform the Division of Child Support (DCS) if my employment changes?

If you pay support pursuant to a DCS wage withholding provision in your order of child support and you change employers, it will be necessary for you to advise DCS of your new employer. You should do this as soon as possible to ensure child support is paid timely and to avoid an *arrearage* (an accumulation of the past child support payments that were not paid by the non-custodial parent of a child in the manner that was ordered by the court), interest charges, and a possible motion for contempt filed by your spouse due to delinquent support. Simply contact your DCS caseworker and advise him or her of the change.

17.3 My order of child support includes a provision requiring my former spouse and me to pay a portion of uninsured medical expenses, child-care expenses, or other expenses incurred for our minor children. How do I track this information and when do I get reimbursed?

Be sure to provide your former spouse with the appropriate documents, as set forth in your decree. Failure to request reimbursement of these expenses in a timely manner may result in collection becoming more difficult. After twenty years, collection is barred under most circumstances. Be sure to keep a copy of all documents sent to the other parent. Maintain complete records regarding these expenses, such as:

- Keeping copies of all billing statements from the service providers with your notations regarding payments made to include the date, amount, and check number
- Keeping copies of all insurance benefits statements
- Asking your pharmacy to give you a monthly or an annual printout of all the charges and payments for prescription drugs

- Asking your child-care provider to give you a monthly or annual printout of all the charges and payments
- Keeping copies of any correspondence between you and the other parent regarding these expenses
- Keeping a record of sums paid by the other parent, either directly to care providers or reimbursements paid to you

Keep these records organized by year and/or by child. You may want to consider creating a worksheet to help you track expenses and payments. In the event of a future dispute, you will then have all of the documentation needed for your attorney to present your case or to defend a claim against you.

17.4 What if my former spouse and I have a disagreement about our parenting plan after the decree is entered?

Most Washington parenting plans provide that future disputes are to be mediated under certain circumstances prior to either party filing a new court action. Ask your attorney if the dispute is one that must be submitted to mediation. If your dispute must be mediated, you still have the right to go back to court and have the judge decide the dispute if mediation was unsuccessful.

If the parenting disagreement is more substantial, you can seek to have the parenting plan clarified by the court or you may seek a modification of the parenting plan. A clarification action provides the parenting plan with more detail. For a modification, Washington case law usually requires showing a substantial change in circumstances in order to modify the residential provisions of most parenting plans. Ask your attorney whether you should seek a clarification or modification of your parenting plan.

17.5 How do I make my court-ordered payments that are not related to child support or spousal maintenance?

If you have been ordered to pay an amount for property settlement, attorney fees, or guardian *ad litem* fees, you should make this payment by check or money order only. Do not ever use cash. It is often helpful to have your attorney send the payment to the other attorney. The payment will be logged in as "copy received," which provides absolute proof of payment.

17.6 My former spouse has not paid me the property settlement as ordered in the decree, what can I do?

In the event that your former spouse does not pay court-ordered judgments, enforcement mechanisms may be available, such as contempt-of-court actions or garnishment. The possibility of non-payment is one reason that you should work with your attorney to obtain "security" for this payment and to protect you from bankruptcy filings. If payment becomes a problem contact your attorney immediately to discuss your enforcement possibilities. It is never wise to wait too long to enforce a delinquency in payment of court-ordered sums.

17.7 After my decree was entered, my former spouse did not pay a judgment and I did not do anything about it. Is it too late?

Judgments for property settlement and/or attorney fees will usually become uncollectable ten years after the date of the judgment. Judgments are formal determinations by a court that one spouse owes the other spouse money. Exceptions may exist, but they are few and rarely applied. Child-support judgments can be extended. Long before your judgment becomes ten years old, see your attorney about pursuing an enforcement action.

17. 8 I restored my former name under my divorce decree, what do I need to do?

The following name-change checklist includes a list of people and places that you may want to contact to let them know your new name. Be prepared to provide these entities with a certified copy of your decree. Many entities will not accept copies of the decree: They must be certified. Your attorney can obtain a certified copy for you or you can obtain your own from the clerk of the court.

_____Banks and other financial institutions

_____Creditors (mortgage company, auto loan companies, credit cards)

_____Credit reporting agencies

_____Department of Motor Vehicles for auto registration

_____Driver's license

_____Deeds and property titles

_____Stock certificates

_____Insurance agencies (homeowner, car, health, life, annuities)

_____Passport office

_____Post office

_____Public assistance office

_____Registrar of voters

_____Schools (yours and your children's)

_____Social Security Administration

_____Utility services (telephone, gas, electric, water, garbage)

17.9   Is there anything else I should be doing after my divorce?

The following post-divorce checklist is helpful in considering many actions that may need to be addressed in your particular circumstances.

Property

_____Confirm necessary quitclaim deeds and real estate transfer statements have been filed with the county.

_____Refinance real property within the time frame specified by decree of dissolution.

_____Complete the exchange of personal property.

_____Transfer the title on vehicles.

_____Transfer or close bank accounts and safe-deposit boxes.

_____Transfer investment accounts, stocks, and bonds.

_____Review beneficiary designations on retirement and financial accounts for any needed changes.

Property Settlement

_____Comply with property settlement payments in a timely manner pursuant to your decree.

What Happens after the Divorce?

Insurance

_____Review life insurance beneficiary designation for any needed changes.

_____Obtain COBRA or other needed health insurance.

_____Notify your medical insurance provider of your divorce.

_____Make sure your vehicle is insured in your name.

_____If you have minor children, inform your attorney if there is any change in the insurance available to them.

Debts and Liabilities

_____Cancel joint accounts or charge cards, or remove the name of your former spouse.

Parenting Plan

_____Notify your child's school of the noncustodial parent's address.

_____If you are the noncustodial parent, notify child's school of your desire to be notified of events, receive duplicate copies of report cards, etc.

Child Support and Maintenance

_____If ordered to pay support, provide the Division of Child Support (DCS) with your employment information. DCS will also collect maintenance if it is collecting child support.

_____If paying or receiving support through DCS, contact DCS if you have a change of address.

Child Care and Uninsured Medical Expenses

_____Set up a tracking-and-filing system to keep full and complete records regarding these financial matters.

Tax Matters

_____Notify your employer of the change in your exemption status (complete a new W-4).

_____Refer to IRS Publication 504, "Divorced or Separated Individuals" for other questions.

Attorney Fees

_____Contact the firm's account manager to make payment arrangements for any fees owed to the firm.

_____If your former spouse was ordered to pay a portion of your attorney fees, note that you remain responsible for the payment of your attorney fees, including any applicable interest, until the account is paid.

_____If you have been ordered to pay fees to your former spouse's attorney, make payment as ordered. If you cannot make the payment on time, contact that attorney's office to try to arrange alternate payment plans.

Name Change

If your name changed:

_____Contact the Social Security Administration (SSA) to complete an Application for Social Security Card (Form SS-5). The SSA will notify the IRS of your name change when your new Social Security card is issued.

_____Notify people and places regarding your name change.

Estate Planning

_____Review your will and any powers of attorney for any needed changes.

_____Schedule an appointment with your attorney to update or prepare your will, powers of attorney, and other important estate planning documents.

In Closing

Now, pause and take a deep breath. Acknowledge yourself for the courage you have shown in examining your unique situation, needs, and goals. You are now facing your future, recasting yourself into a new life. You are looking more closely at your living situation, the needs of your children, your financial security, and your own personal growth and healing. You are taking action to propel yourself into new possibilities.

From here, it is time to take inventory of the lessons learned, goals met, and actions yet to be taken. Celebrate each step forward and be gentle with yourself over the occasional misstep. You have transitioned through an exceptionally difficult time. With every day that passes following the completion of your divorce, your grief will begin to subside and your energy will begin to improve as you move toward a fresh start. All the best to you as you accomplish this life journey!

Appendix

Sample Parenting Plan

Superior Court of Washington
County of

☐ In re the Marriage of:
☐ In re the Domestic Partnership of:

Petitioner,	**No.**
and	**Parenting Plan**
	☐ **Proposed (PPP)**
	☐ **Temporary (PPT)**
Respondent.	☐ **Final Order (PP)**

This parenting plan is:

☐ the final parenting plan signed by the court pursuant to a decree of dissolution, legal separation, or declaration concerning validity signed by the court on this date or dated _____.

☐ the final parenting plan signed by the court pursuant to an order signed by the court on this date or dated _____, which modifies a previous parenting plan or custody decree.

☐ a temporary parenting plan signed by the court.

proposed by (name) _____.

It Is Ordered, Adjudged and Decreed:

I. General Information

This parenting plan applies to the following children:

Name   Age

_____   _____

_____   _____

_____   _____

II. Basis for Restrictions

Under certain circumstances, as outlined below, the court may limit or prohibit a parent's contact with the child(ren) and the right to make decisions for the child(ren).

2.1   Parental Conduct (RCW 26.09.191(1), (2))

☐   Does not apply.

☐   The ☐ petitioner's ☐ respondent's residential time with the child(ren) shall be limited or restrained completely, and mutual decision-making and designation of a dispute resolution process other than court action shall not be required, because ☐ this parent ☐ a person residing with this parent has engaged in the conduct which follows:

☐   Willful abandonment that continues for an extended period of time or substantial refusal to perform parenting functions (this applies only to parents, not to a person who resides with a parent).

☐   Physical, sexual or a pattern of emotional abuse of a child.

☐   A history of acts of domestic violence as defined in RCW 26.50.010(1) or an assault or sexual assault which causes grievous bodily harm or the fear of such harm.

2.2   Other Factors (RCW 26.09.191(3))

☐   Does not apply.

☐   The ☐ petitioner's ☐ respondent's involvement or conduct may have an adverse effect on the child(ren)'s best interests because of the existence of the factors which follow:

☐   Neglect or substantial nonperformance of parenting functions.

216

☐   A long-term emotional or physical impairment which interferes with the performance of parenting functions as defined in RCW 26.09.004.

☐   A long-term impairment resulting from drug, alcohol, or other substance abuse that interferes with the performance of parenting functions.

☐   The absence or substantial impairment of emotional ties between the parent and child.

☐   The abusive use of conflict by the parent which creates the danger of serious damage to the child's psychological development.

☐   A parent has withheld from the other parent access to the child for a protracted period without good cause.

☐   Other:

III. Residential Schedule

The residential schedule must set forth where the child(ren) shall reside each day of the year, including provisions for holidays, birthdays of family members, vacations, and other special occasions, and what contact the child(ren) shall have with each parent. Parents are encouraged to create a residential schedule that meets the developmental needs of the child(ren) and individual needs of their family. Paragraphs 3.1 through 3.9 are one way to write your residential schedule. If you do not use these paragraphs, write in your own schedule in Paragraph 3.13.

3.1   Schedule for Children Under School Age

☐   There are no children under school age.

☐   Prior to enrollment in school, the child(ren) shall reside with the ☐ petitioner ☐ respondent, except for the following days and times when the child(ren) will reside with or be with the other parent:

from (day and time)_____ to (day and time) _____

    ☐   every week ☐ every other week ☐ the first and third week of the month

    ☐   the second and fourth week of the month ☐ other:

from (day and time)_____to (day and time) _____

    ☐   every week ☐ every other week ☐ the first and third week of the month

    ☐   the second and fourth week of the month [ ] other:

3.2   School Schedule

Upon enrollment in school, the child(ren) shall reside with the ☐ petitioner ☐ respondent, except for the following days and times when the child(ren) will reside with or be with the other parent:

from (day and time)_____to (day and time) _____

    ☐ every week ☐ every other week ☐ the first and third week of the month

    ☐ the second and fourth week of the month ☐ other:

from (day and time)_____to (day and time) _____

    ☐ every week ☐ every other week ☐ the first and third week of the month

    ☐ the second and fourth week of the month ☐ other:

☐ The school schedule will start when each child begins ☐ kindergarten ☐ first grade ☐ other:

3.3   Schedule for Winter Vacation

The child(ren) shall reside with the ☐ petitioner ☐ respondent during winter vacation, except for the following days and times when the child(ren) will reside with or be with the other parent:

3.4   Schedule for Other School Breaks

The child(ren) shall reside with the ☐ petitioner ☐ respondent during other school breaks, except for the following days and times when the child(ren) will reside with or be with the other parent:

3.5   Summer Schedule

Upon completion of the school year, the child(ren) shall reside with the ☐ petitioner ☐ respondent, except for the following days and times when the child(ren) will reside with or be with the other parent:

    ☐ Same as school year schedule.

    ☐ Other:

3.6 Vacation With Parents

☐ Does not apply.

☐ The schedule for vacation with parents is as follows:

3.7 Schedule for Holidays

The residential schedule for the child(ren) for the holidays listed below is as follows:

	With Petitioner (Specify Year Odd/Even/Every)	With Respondent (Specify Year Odd/Even/Every)
New Year's Day		
Martin Luther King Day		
Presidents' Day		
Memorial Day		
July 4th		
Labor Day		
Veterans' Day		
Thanksgiving Day		
Christmas Eve		
Christmas Day		

☐ For purposes of this parenting plan, a holiday shall begin and end as follows (set forth times):

☐ Holidays which fall on a Friday or a Monday shall include Saturday and Sunday.

☐ Other:

3.8 Schedule for Special Occasions

The residential schedule for the child(ren) for the following special occasions (for example, birthdays) is as follows:

	With Petitioner (Specify Year Odd/Even/Every)	With Respondent (Specify Year Odd/Even/Every)
Mother's Day		
Father's Day		

☐ Other:

3.9   Priorities Under the Residential Schedule

☐   Does not apply because one parent has no visitation or restricted visitation.

☐   Paragraphs 3.3—3.8, have priority over paragraphs 3.1 and 3.2, in the following order:

    ☐   Rank the order of priority, with 1 being given the highest priority:

    ____winter vacation (3.3)   ____holidays (3.7)
    ____school breaks (3.4)   ____special occasions (3.8)
    ____summer schedule (3.5)   ____vacation with parents (3.6)

☐   Other:

3.10 Restrictions

☐   Does not apply because there are no limiting factors in paragraphs 2.1 or 2.2.

☐   The ☐ petitioner's ☐ respondent's residential time with the children shall be limited because there are limiting factors in paragraphs 2.1 and 2.2. The following restrictions shall apply when the children spend time with this parent:

☐   There are limiting factors in paragraph 2.2, but there are no restrictions on the ☐ petitioner's ☐ respondent's residential time with the children for the following reasons:

3.11 Transportation Arrangements

Transportation costs are included in the Child Support Worksheets and/or the Order of Child Support and should not be included here.
Transportation arrangements for the child(ren), between parents shall be as follows:

3.12 Designation of Custodian

The children named in this parenting plan are scheduled to reside the majority of the time with the ☐ petitioner ☐ respondent. This parent is designated the custodian of the child(ren) solely for purposes of all other state and federal statutes which require a designation or determination of custody. This designation shall not affect either parent's rights and responsibilities under this parenting plan.

3.13 Other

3.14 Summary of RCW 26.09.430 - .480, Regarding Relocation of a Child

This is a summary only. For the full text, please see RCW 26.09.430 through 26.09.480.

If the person with whom the child resides a majority of the time plans to move, that person shall give notice to every person entitled to court ordered time with the child.

If the move is outside the child's school district, the relocating person must give notice by personal service or by mail requiring a return receipt. This notice must be at least 60 days before the intended move. If the relocating person could not have known about the move in time to give 60 days' notice, that person must give notice within 5 days after learning of the move. The notice must contain the information required in RCW 26.09.440. See also form DRPSCU 07.0500, (Notice of Intended Relocation of A Child).

If the move is within the same school district, the relocating person must provide actual notice by any reasonable means. A person entitled to time with the child may not object to the move but may ask for modification under RCW 26.09.260.

Notice may be delayed for 21 days if the relocating person is entering a domestic violence shelter or is moving to avoid a clear, immediate and unreasonable risk to health and safety.

If information is protected under a court order or the address confidentiality program, it may be withheld from the notice.

A relocating person may ask the court to waive any notice requirements that may put the health and safety of a person or a child at risk.

Failure to give the required notice may be grounds for sanctions, including contempt.

If no objection is filed within 30 days after service of the notice of intended relocation, the relocation will be permitted and the proposed revised residential schedule may be confirmed.

A person entitled to time with a child under a court order can file an objection to the child's relocation whether or not he or she received proper notice.

An objection may be filed by using the mandatory pattern form WPF DRPSCU 07.0700, (Objection to Relocation/Petition for Modification of Custody Decree/Parenting Plan/Residential Schedule). The objection must be served on all persons entitled to time with the child.

The relocating person shall not move the child during the time for objection unless: (a) the delayed notice provisions apply; or (b) a court order allows the move.

If the objecting person schedules a hearing for a date within 15 days of timely service of the objection, the relocating person shall not move the child before the hearing unless there is a clear, immediate and unreasonable risk to the health or safety of a person or a child.

IV. Decision Making

4.1 Day-to-Day Decisions

Each parent shall make decisions regarding the day-to-day care and control of each child while the child is residing with that parent. Regardless of the allocation of decision making in this parenting plan, either parent may make emergency decisions affecting the health or safety of the children.

4.2 Major Decisions

Major decisions regarding each child shall be made as follows:

Education decisions ☐ petitioner ☐ respondent ☐ joint
Non-emergency health care ☐ petitioner ☐ respondent ☐ joint
Religious upbringing ☐ petitioner ☐ respondent ☐ joint
_____ ☐ petitioner ☐ respondent ☐ joint
_____ ☐ petitioner ☐ respondent ☐ joint
_____ ☐ petitioner ☐ respondent ☐ joint

4.3 Restrictions in Decision Making

☐   Does not apply because there are no limiting factors in paragraphs 2.1 and 2.2 above.

☐   Sole decision making shall be ordered to the ☐ petitioner ☐ respondent for the following reasons:

Appendix

☐ A limitation on the other parent's decision making authority is mandated by RCW 26.09.191 (See paragraph 2.1).

☐ Both parents are opposed to mutual decision making.

☐ One parent is opposed to mutual decision making, and such opposition is reasonably based on the following criteria:

(a) The existence of a limitation under RCW 26.09.191;

(b) The history of participation of each parent in decision making in each of the areas in RCW 26.09.184(4)(a);

(c) Whether the parents have demonstrated ability and desire to cooperate with one another in decision making in each of the areas in RCW 26.09.184(4) (a); and

(d) The parents' geographic proximity to one another, to the extent that it affects their ability to make timely mutual decisions.

☐ There are limiting factors in paragraph 2.2, but there are no restrictions on mutual decision making for the following reasons:

V. Dispute Resolution

The purpose of this dispute resolution process is to resolve disagreements about carrying out this parenting plan. This dispute resolution process may, and under some local court rules or the provisions of this plan, must be used before filing a petition to modify the plan or a motion for contempt for failing to follow the plan.

☐ Disputes between the parties, other than child support disputes, shall be submitted to (list person or agency):

☐ counseling by_____, or

☐ mediation by_____, if this box is checked and issues of domestic violence or child abuse are present, then the court finds that the victim requested mediation, that mediation is appropriate and that the victim is permitted to have a supporting person present during the mediation proceedings, or

☐ arbitration by_____.

The cost of this process shall be allocated between the parties as follows:

    ☐ _____% petitioner _____% respondent.

    ☐ based on each party's proportional share of income from line 6 of the child support worksheets.

    ☐ as determined in the dispute resolution process.

The dispute resolution process shall be commenced by notifying the other party by ☐ written request ☐ certified mail ☐ other:

In the dispute resolution process:

    (a) Preference shall be given to carrying out this Parenting Plan.

    (b) Unless an emergency exists, the parents shall use the designated process to resolve disputes relating to implementation of the plan, except those related to financial support.

    (c) A written record shall be prepared of any agreement reached in counseling or mediation and of each arbitration award and shall be provided to each party.

    (d) If the court finds that a parent has used or frustrated the dispute resolution process without good reason, the court shall award attorneys' fees and financial sanctions to the other parent.

    (e) The parties have the right of review from the dispute resolution process to the superior court.

☐   No dispute resolution process, except court action is ordered.

VI. Other Provisions

☐   There are no other provisions.

☐   There are the following other provisions:

VII. Declaration for Proposed Parenting Plan

☐   Does not apply.

☐   (Only sign if this is a proposed parenting plan.) I declare under penalty of perjury under the laws of the state of Washington

Appendix

that this plan has been proposed in good faith and that the statements in Part II of this Plan are true and correct.

_____   _____
Petitioner   Date and Place of Signature

_____   _____
Respondent   Date and Place of Signature

VIII. Order by the Court

It is ordered, adjudged and decreed that the parenting plan set forth above is adopted and approved as an order of this court.

WARNING: Violation of residential provisions of this order with actual knowledge of its terms is punishable by contempt of court and may be a criminal offense under RCW 9A.40.060(2) or 9A.40.070(2). Violation of this order may subject a violator to arrest.

When mutual decision making is designated but cannot be achieved, the parties shall make a good faith effort to resolve the issue through the dispute resolution process.

If a parent fails to comply with a provision of this plan, the other parent's obligations under the plan are not affected.

Dated:_____   _____
                                                    Judge/Commissioner

Presented by: Approved for entry:

_____   _____
Signature of Party or Lawyer/WSBA No. Signature of Party or Lawyer/WSBA No.

_____   _____
Print Name   Print Name

Resources

Annual Credit Report Request Service
P.O. Box 105283
Atlanta, GA 30348-5283
Phone: (877) 322–8228
www.annualcreditreport.com
This website offers a centralized service for consumers to request annual credit reports. It was created by the three nationwide consumer credit reporting companies, Equifax, Experian, and TransUnion. AnnualCreditReport.com processes requests for free credit file disclosures (commonly called credit reports). Under the Fair and Accurate Credit Transactions Act (FACT Act), consumers can request and obtain a free credit report once every twelve months from each of the three nationwide consumer credit reporting companies. AnnualCreditReport.com offers consumers a fast and convenient way to request, view, and print their credit reports in a secure Internet environment. It also provides options to request reports by telephone and by mail.

Gonzaga University School of Law Clinic
www.law.gonzaga.edu/academics/law-clinic/legal-help/
Phone: (509) 313-5791

Internal Revenue Service (IRS)
www.irs.gov
Phone: (800) 829-1040 for individual tax questions
(800) 829-4933 for business tax questions.
The IRS website allows you to search for any keyword, review publications and information on tax questions, or submit a question via e-mail or phone to an IRS representative.

King County Court Family Law Facilitator
516 Third Avenue, Room W-382
Seattle, Washington 98104
Phone: (206) 296-9092
www.kingcounty.gov/courts/FamilyCourt/facilitator.aspx

Moderate Means Program
www.moderatemeanswa.org
Phone: (855) 741-6930
The Moderate Means Program is a partnership between the Washington State Bar Association and Washington's three law schools. The Program connects people within 200 to 400 percent of the federal poverty level to lawyers who offer family, housing, and consumer legal help at reduced fees.

Northwest Justice Project
http://nwjustice.org/
Phone: (888) 201-1014
Northwest Justice Project offers low-cost legal advice or representation to low-income populations. It has offices throughout the state of Washington. Please see the website for specific contact information for your location.

Office of Civil Legal Aid
www.ocla.wa.gov
1112 Quince Street S.E.
P.O. Box 41183
Olympia, WA 98504-1183
Phone: (360) 704-4135

Resources

Seattle University School of Law Clinic
www.law.seattleu.edu/academics/law-clinic
Phone: (206) 398-4130
This clinic offer legal assistance on civil matters to low-income populations. In addition to providing a service to the community, the clinic also provides a learning environment for Gonzaga, UW, and Seattle University law students. It operates as a small law firm staffed by law students under the supervision of faculty members.

Social Security Administration
Office of Public Inquiries
Windsor Park Building
6401 Security Boulevard
Baltimore, MD 21235
Phone: (800) 772-1213
www.ssa.gov
The website enables users to search for a question or word, submit questions via e-mail, or review recent publications.

Spokane County Court Family Law Facilitator
Family Law Center
1116 W. Broadway, Room 101
Spokane, WA 99260-0350
Phone: (509) 477-7612
The Family Law Facilitator Program provides information and referrals to family law litigants who are not represented by attorneys. Litigants may meet with a facilitator on a walk-in basis (walk-ins are first come, first served, and sign-in will end thirty minutes prior to closing or once capacity is reached) or by prescheduled appointment (for document review or if an interpreter is required). Please see your local court website for more information.

University of Washington Law School Clinic
www.law.washington.edu/clinics/clients.aspx

Washington Law Help
www.washingtonlawhelp.org/issues/family-law

Washington State Coalition Against Domestic Violence
500 Union Street, Suite 200
Seattle, WA 98101
Phone: (206) 389-2515
www.wscadv.org

The Washington State Coalition Against Domestic Violence is a statewide advocacy organization committed to the prevention and elimination of sexual and domestic violence. WSCADV works to enhance safety and justice for victims of domestic violence and sexual assault by supporting and building upon the services provided by the network of local programs. The coalition also has offices in Olympia.

Washington State Department of Social and Health Services
Division of Child Support
P.O. Box 11520
Tacoma, WA 98411-5520
Phone: (360) 664-3210 or toll free (800) 922-4306
http://dshs.wa.gov/dcs/

This site includes specific sections for individuals receiving support, individuals paying support, and for employers of individuals paying support. Information related to payment can be found at this website. A toll-free automated system to check on the status of the receipt and disbursement of child support, as well as any outstanding balance owed, can be accessed.

Glossary

Affidavit: A written statement of facts made under oath and signed before a notary public. Affidavits are used primarily when there will not be a hearing in open court with live testimony. The attorney will prepare an affidavit to present relevant facts. Affidavits may be signed by the parties or in some cases by witnesses. A "declaration" is a similar document, completed under penalty of perjury but not signed before a notary public. Both documents are usually acceptable in Washington family law cases.

Answer: A written response to the petition for divorce. It serves to admit or deny the allegations in the complaint and may also make claims against the opposing party. In family law, this is usually referred to as a "Responsive to Petition." An answer must be timely filed, usually within twenty days of service if served within Washington, or within sixty days of service if served outside of Washington.

Appeal: The process by which a higher court reviews the decision of a lower court. In Washington family law cases, a person will first file an appeal with the Washington Court of Appeals. After that appeal is decided, there may be a further appeal to the Washington Supreme Court.

Child support: Financial support for a child paid by the noncustodial parent to the custodial parent.

Court order: A court-issued document setting forth the judge's orders. An order can be issued based upon the parties' agreement or the judge's decision. An order may require the parties to perform certain acts or set forth their rights and responsibilities. An order is put in writing, signed by the judge, and filed with the court.

Contempt of court: The willful and intentional failure of a party to comply with a court order, judgment, or decree. Contempt may be punishable by a fine or jail.

Contested case: Any case in which the parties cannot reach an agreement. A contested case will result in a trial to have the judge decide disputed issues.

Cross-examination: The questioning of a witness by the opposing counsel during trial or at a deposition, in response to questions asked by the other attorney.

Custody: The legal right and responsibility awarded by a court for the possession of, care of, and decision making for a minor child.

Decree of dissolution: A final court order dissolving the marriage, dividing property and debts, ordering support, and entering other orders regarding finances and the minor children.

Deposition: A witness's testimony taken out of court, under oath, and in the presence of attorneys and a court reporter. If a person gives a different testimony at the time of trial, he or she can be impeached with the deposition testimony; that is, statements made at a deposition can be used to show untruthfulness if a different answer is given at trial.

Direct examination: The initial questioning of a witness in court by the attorney who called him or her to the stand.

Discovery: A process used by attorneys to discover information from the opposing party for the purpose of fully assessing a case for settlement or trial. Types of discovery include interrogatories, requests for production of documents, and requests for admissions.

Dissolution: The act of terminating or dissolving a marriage.

Equitable distribution of property: The method by which real and personal property and debts are divided in a divorce. Given all economic circumstances of the parties, Washington law requires that marital property and debts be divided in a fair and reasonable manner.

Ex parte: Usually in reference to a motion, the term used to describe an appearance of only one party before the judge, without the other party being present. For example, an *ex parte* restraining order may be granted immediately after the filing of a petition for divorce.

Glossary

Guardian *ad litem* (GAL): A person, often an attorney or mental health professional, appointed by court to conduct an investigation regarding the children's best interests.

Hearing: Any proceeding before the court for the purpose of resolving disputed issues between the parties through presentation of testimony, affidavits, declarations, exhibits, or argument.

Hold-harmless clause: A term in a court order that requires one party to assume responsibility for a debt and to protect the other spouse from any loss or expense in connection with it, as in to hold harmless from liability.

Interrogatories: Written questions under oath sent from one party to the other that are used to obtain facts or opinions related to the divorce.

Joint custody: The equally shared right and responsibility of both parents awarded by the court for residential time with the children.

Maintenance: Court-ordered spousal support payments from one party to another, often to enable the recipient spouse to become economically independent.

Mediation: A process by which a neutral third party facilitates negotiations between the parties on a wide range of issues.

Modification: A party's written request to the court to change a prior order regarding custody, child support, maintenance, or any other order that the court may change by law.

Motion: A written application to the court for relief, such as temporary child support, custody, or restraining orders.

No-fault divorce: The type of divorce Washington has where the court does not require evidence of marital misconduct. This means that abandonment, cruelty, and adultery are neither relevant nor required to be proven for the purposes of granting the divorce.

Notice of hearing: A written statement sent to the opposing attorney or spouse listing the date and place of a hearing and the nature of the matters that will be heard by the court. In Washington, one party is required to give the other party reasonable notice of any court hearing unless an emergency exists.

Party: The person in a legal action whose rights or interests will be affected by the divorce. For example, in a divorce, the parties include the wife and husband.

Pending: During the case. For example, the judge may award you temporary support while your case is pending.

Petition: The first document filed with the clerk of the court, along with the summons, in an action for divorce, separation, or paternity. The petition sets forth the facts on which the requested relief is based.

Petitioner: A term formally used to refer to the person who files the petition seeking a divorce.

Pleadings: Documents filed with the court.

Qualified Domestic Relations Order (QDRO): A type of court order that provides for direct payment from a retirement account to a former spouse.

Request for production of documents: A written request for documents sent from one party to the other during the discovery process.

Respondent: The responding party to a divorce; the party who did not file the petition initiating the divorce.

Set off: A debt or financial obligation of one spouse that is deducted from the debt or financial obligation of the other spouse.

Settlement: The agreed resolution of disputed issues.

Show cause: Written application to the court to hold another person in contempt of court for violating or failing to comply with a current court order.

Stipulation: An agreement reached between parties or an agreement by their attorneys.

Subpoena: A document delivered to a person or witness that requires him or her to appear in court, appear for a deposition, or produce documents. Failure to comply could result in punishment by the court. A subpoena requesting documents is called a subpoena *duces tecum.*

Temporary restraining order (TRO): An order of the court prohibiting a party from certain behavior. For example, a temporary restraining order may order a person not to transfer any funds during a pending divorce action.

Trial: A formal court hearing in which the judge will decide disputed issues raised by the parties' pleadings.

Under advisement: A term used to describe the status of a case, usually after a court hearing on a motion or a trial, when the judge has not yet made a decision.

Index

Index

competition, 25
Confidential Information form, 37
confidentiality, 23, 38–39, 63
conflict with spouse, 74, 116
confusion during divorce process, 30–31
contempt-of-court, 209
contingency fees, 51–52
continuances of court, 191
cost-of-living allowance (COLA), 169
costs, *see* fees
counseling, 27, 101–102
counselor, role in child custody, 108
county and residential requirements, 7–8
court, *see also* trial
appearing in, 189–190
bailiff's role in, 193
case scheduling order and, 195
child/children in, 99, 102
child support, picking up from, 128
contempt-of-, 209
continuances of, 191
court reporter's role in, 193–194
dates for, 189
emotional breakdown during, 29–30
etiquette during, 192–193
factors determining occurrence of, 189–190
going to, 188–201
Indian tribal, 8–9
judge's role in, 201
payments ordered by, 208–209
personal support in, 198–199
preparing for, 29–30, 196
pretrial conference prior to, 195–196
questions asked by attorney

during, 194–195
settlement agreement and going to, 192
spouse's attendance in, 190, 198
talking to attorney during, 194
temporary hearings in, 191–192
testifying in, 191
court commissioners, 192
court order, *see also* specific types of
for attorney fees, 63
ex parte, 14
for parenting time, 114
protection, 86–88
temporary, 15, 45, 97–98, 203
wage-withholding, 129
court reporter, 55, 193–194
credit cards, 173–175, 176
cross-examination, 200
custody, *see* child custody

D

dates for court, 189
dating and child custody, 103–104
death, 140, 162, 169
debts, division of, 172–180
bankruptcy and, 178–180
credit cards, 173–175, 176
division of property and, 161
during divorce process, 176
hold-harmless clause and, 177
medical bills, 177–178
mortgage, 173–174, 178
premarital debt and, 177
spouse, liability for debt of, 176
student loans, 175–176
"decision-making" section of parenting plan, 111
decree, 37, *see also* finality of divorce
decree of dissolution of

Index

trial, and preparing for, 19
domestic violence, 86–90, 97,
   114–116

E

education, 96, 133–134
e-mail, 39, 57, 82
emergencies, 85–93
  abduction, 90–91
  abuse, 86, 89–90
  bank accounts, emptying of,
    89
  desertion, 85
  domestic violence, 86–88, 89–
    90
  harassment, 89
  home, temporary possession
    of, 92–93
  information provided to attor-
    ney about, 87
  involving child/children, 86,
    91
  protection orders for, 87–88
  restraining order for, 87–88
emotional breakdown during
  court, 29–30
emotional relationship with
  child/children, 96
Employee's Withholding
  Certificate, 186, *see also* IRS
  Form W-4
employment, informing court of
  changes in, 207
employment retirement benefits,
  see retirement
engagement ring, 156
Equifax, 174
equitable right of
  reimbursement, 155
equity of house/home, 145,
  146–147
ethics of attorney, 23
etiquette during court, 192–193
evaluation fees, 55
ex parte court order, 14

Experian, 174
expert-witness fees, 55

F

Facebook, 39, 109
Fair Credit Reporting Act, 174
family, see personal support
family law attorney, 33
fearing spouse, see
  emergencies
fee advance, 52
fees, 51–56, 76, 81, *see also*
  attorney fees
  for appeals process, 205
  guardian *ad litem*, 55, 208–209
  for property settlement agree-
    ment, 208–209
  taxes, deducting for, 186
filing for divorce, 9–11, 55, 89
filing status for taxes, 183
finality of divorce, 11, 21
finances/financing, 15, 62,
  151–154
financial declaration form, 136
flat rate attorney fees, 27, 52
foreign country, 92
former name, legal restoration
  of, 21, 209–210
401(k) retirement plan, 153, 166,
  174, 186
403(b) retirement plan, 186
free attorney, 2
free initial consultation, 49–50
free legal advice, 49–50
friends, see personal support
furniture, 149

G

garnishment, 209
gay parents, 105
general expenses, 132
gifts, 154–156
Gmail, 39
goodwill valuation, 158
grounds for divorce, 5
guardian *ad litem*

Index

Index

with, 45–48
fees for, 57
mediation and negotiation, role
in, 78
utilizing, 60

T

talking about divorce with child/
children, 24
talking to attorney during court,
194
taxes, 181–187
on alimony, 138–139, 182–183
childcare tax credit for, 185
children as dependents for
purpose of, 185
on child support, 181–182
discovery process for, 184
fees for divorce, deducting for,
186
filing status for, 183
innocent spouse relief for, 187
IRS Form 8332 for, 185
IRS Form W-4 for, 186
joint income tax return for, 183
property settlement agreement
and, 181
property transfer and, 181
on real estate, 184–185
on retirement plan, 186
telephone calls, 43, 49–50, 57,
60, 82
temporary child support, 123
temporary court order, 15, 45,
97–98, 203
temporary hearing, 15, 191–192
temporary restraining order
(TRO), 88
"tender years" doctrine, 96
term life insurance, 170
testifying/testimony, 70, 191,
199
therapy and child custody,
101–102
transferring assets, 148–149

transitions, 30–31
TransUnion, 174
travel during parenting time,
out-of-state/country, 118–119
trial, 197–200, *see also* court
anxiety and, 1
attorney fees for, 58–59
documents and preparing for,
19
trust, 83
truth during deposition, 71
Twitter, 39

U

unfit parent, 110
Uniform Child Custody
Jurisdiction Enforcement Act
(UCCJEA), 91
uninsured medical expenses, 48,
132, 207–208

V

vacation, summer, 129
valuation of goodwill, 158
value of house/home, 144–145,
147
vehicles, 149, 173, 174
video to help determine child
custody, 108–109
Violence Against Women Act, 8
visitation, 97
Vital Statistics form, 37
voluntarily paying child support,
124

W

wage garnishment, 209
wage-withholding order, 129
waiting period for divorce, 9
Washington Child Support
Guidelines, 122, 124–125
Washington Court of Appeals,
41, 203
Washington Court Rules, 66
Washington Supreme Court, 41,
154

About the Author

David J. Crouse is the founding partner of David J. Crouse & Associates, PLLC. His career has focused exclusively on family law-related work. David has been published in the Gonzaga University Law Review and in other publications. He is a frequent lecturer at Washington family law-related continuing legal education courses. David has been elected to the Order of Barristers for excellence in courtroom advocacy. He has received multiple American Jurisprudence awards for legal writing and oral advocacy. He has served as a Superior Court judge *pro tem*.

David earned his bachelor of arts degree from Gonzaga University and went on to obtain his law degree, with honors, from Gonzaga University School of Law in 1993. While at Gonzaga University School of Law, David won the client counseling competition and the Linden Cup Competition. The Linden Cup is a competition to determine the best oral advocate in the law school. Following Linden Cup, David competed in National Moot Court against all other United States law schools. He, along with his partners, received the "best legal brief in the nation" recognition and finished second in the nation in oral advocacy.

David's firm website can be found at:
www.crouselawgroup.com.

Divorce Titles from Addicus Books

Visit our online catalog at www.AddicusBooks.com

To Order Books:
Visit us online at: www.AddicusBooks.com
Call toll free: (800) 888-4741

Addicus Books
P. O. Box 45327
Omaha, NE 68145

*Addicus Books is dedicated to publishing books
that comfort and educate.*